FOURSCORE AND 7

Betsy Franco

FOURSCORE AND 7

Betsy Franco

Good Year Books

ACKNOWLEDGMENTS

Writing a book such as *Fourscore and Seven* requires all types of support, from technical to emotional.

The reference librarians at the Palo Alto Main Library cheerfully helped me research the minutiae necessary for an American history book involving mathematics. Maria Damon and Lorraine Bates Noyes were invaluable resources for gender and multicultural issues, and Jim Bertsch generously brainstormed ideas with me at Little League games.

My husband Doug, who has a vast knowledge of history and math offered me intriguing perspectives on traditional issues in American history. I also felt support from my father who was a history buff, but a self-described "terrible mathematician."

Finally, I am grateful to the students in my social studies and mathematics classes, from elementary to high school. I thank them for their feedback on my ideas over the years.

Good Year Books

are available for most basic curriculum subjects plus many enrichment areas. For more Good Year Books, contact your local bookseller or educational dealer. For a complete catalog with information about other Good Year Books, please visit: www.goodyearbooks.com.

Good Year Books
P.O. Box 91858
Tucson, AZ 85752-1858

Book design by Karen Kohn and Associates, Ltd.
Cover illustration and interior line art illustrations by Susan Swan.
Chapter opener illustrations by Karen Kohn and Associates, Ltd.
Copyright © 1999 Good Year Books
All Rights Reserved.
Printed in the United States of America.

1-59647-000-3
2 3 4 5 6 7 8 9 - ML - 08 07 06 05 04

GOOD YEAR BOOKS

PREFACE

How many students know what *fourscore* actually means in the Gettysburg Address? Numbers abound in American history — numbers that not only help students grasp historical concepts but also enable them to grapple with higher level mathematics. Once I realized the power of the numbers embedded in American history, I decided to start at the beginning of the country's history and see where it took me. It took me to the Boston Tea Party Museum to find out the size of tea chests. It took me to a covered wagon tour guide who could measure and weigh the wheels and the axle on his covered wagons. It took me to the National Bison Association to estimate the number of buffalo left in North America.

I found that U. S. history is a rich source of mathematics that has not been thoroughly tapped. *Fourscore and Seven* does just that by integrating history and math through project-based learning. Students are given the opportunity to explore particular slices of American history in great depth. By solving intriguing, open-ended mathematical problems, they can relive the emotions and appreciate the "nitty-gritty" details that give history its meaning and make it memorable.

The activities in *Fourscore and Seven* span the period from before the explorers to current events. As the history progresses, the math progresses. The math includes geometry, factors and primes, operations with large numbers, fractions, decimals, measurement, area and volume, probability, discrete math, ratio and scale, data and graphing, and percent.

Throughout the book, I have emphasized multicultural and gender issues. I believe that every student needs to see herself or himself represented in American history.

How to Use This Book

The chapters in *Fourscore and Seven* are intended to supplement the math and social studies curricula by offering a way to look at traditional material from a different vantage point. All of the research has been done; the chapters are self-contained. You need only fit the material into your curriculum. If you are a math or social studies teacher in a middle-school setting, you can use the chapters to coordinate your teaching.

Since *Fourscore and Seven* spans grades 5–8, the projects have been written so that you can tailor the challenges to your students. Each challenge includes an extra activity to extend the learning. Project by project, you can decide if this section is appropriate for your students.

What's in Each Chapter?

Teacher Notes

Synopsis of the challenge

Math skills and concepts used

Materials needed

Interesting details for discussion

Possible solutions to the challenge

Questions to ask as students work on the challenge

Student Pages

Introduction to the historical material

Challenge involving math and history, along with an extra extension

Materials needed

The facts students will need

A list of things to do to keep students organized and on task

Implementing Each Chapter

- To begin a chapter, distribute the student pages to pairs or groups of students. Read and discuss the introductory material on the student pages.
- Use the background information in the teacher notes to fill in gaps and to enrich the history.
- Have the class discuss and clarify the challenge and the interesting details. Decide if students should complete the extra challenge or not.
- Let pairs or groups of students work on the challenge, using the To Do List as a guide.
- Circulate among the students, asking the questions to help students focus on the issues and probe more deeply into the challenge.
- Discuss the results as a class.

CONTENTS

1 Weaving with Spider Woman: Navajo Blankets   1

Tessellations; Geometry; Slides, Flips, and Turns

Students create their own Navajo-style blanket on grid paper by tessellating traditional Native American designs.

2 From Triumph to Tragedy: René-Robert Cavalier, Sieur de La Salle, French Explorer   11

Area, Fractions, Map Scale

Students estimate how much land La Salle claimed for the French and what fraction of America that would have been.

3 Did Betsy Ross Really Sew It?: The Stars and Stripes   17

Factors, Primes, Composites, Patterns, Symmetry, Algebra (optional)

Students design flags in American history and use them to explore factors, primes, and composites.

4 Blending African and American Traditions: African American Quilters   29

Geometry, Fractions

Students create African American-inspired quilts. They use friendly fractions to find what fraction of the quilt is covered by each color.

5 Sheepes Tongue Pie: A Selection of Colonial Recipes   35

Adding and Multiplying Fractions

Students use traditional recipes to answer fractional questions and to adjust recipes to feed the whole class.

6 "Boston Harbor a teapot tonight!": The Boston Tea Party   43

Length, Weight, Area, Volume; Multiplying and Dividing Large Numbers

Students use facts about the Boston Tea Party to find out about how many pounds of tea were dumped and how much floor space the tea would have taken up in their classroom.

7 From Licorice to Button Hooks: Shopping at a General Store   51
Operations with Decimals (Money)
Students place orders using a price list from a general store in colonial times.

8 Wagons Ho!: Packing a Covered Wagon   59
Weight, Volume, Circumference; Scale
Given the volume of a covered wagon and the volume and weight of typical household goods, students decide what they would have taken with them.

9 Home on the Range: The American Buffalo   69
Large Numbers, Visual Representation of Data, Proportion
Students create visuals showing the changes in the buffalo population over the years.

10 Eureka!: The California Gold Rush   77
Probability
Students create games of chance with a Gold Rush theme.

11 A "Train" to Freedom: The Underground Railroad   87
Discrete Mathematics, Routing
Students use discrete math to find how many possible routes on particular maps of the Underground Railroad.

12 The Mail Must Go Through: The Pony Express   95
Ratio, Rate, Scale
Students plan a reenactment of the Pony Express by assigning classmates to parts of the route, using a map and facts about speed and endurance.

13 Lady Liberty: Immigration and the Statue of Liberty   101
Ratio, Scale, Fractions
Students use their own measurements and proportions to estimate lengths on the Statue of Liberty.

14 Battle at the Ballot Box: Women and the Right to Vote   109

Fractions, Decimals, Percent

Students figure out the fraction and/or percent of the states that gave women the right to vote before 1920.

15 "I Do Solemnly Swear . . .": Presidents of the United States   117

Making and Interpreting Graphs

Students study statistics about the presidents and create bar graphs using the data.

16 Which Faces Do You Recognize?: Current Events   131

Percents

Students cut out newspaper and magazine pictures of people who are affecting American history today. After trying to identify these people, each student calculates his or her percentage of correct answers.

Bibliography   135

CHAPTER 1
Weaving with Spider Woman

NAVAJO BLANKETS

Weaving with Spider Woman
NAVAJO BLANKETS

The Challenge

Students figure out which traditional Navajo designs will tessellate by themselves. Then they create a Navajo-style blanket on grid paper by tessellating several of the designs.

Extra: Students record the slides, flips, and turns they used when tessellating designs on their blankets.

Math Skills/Concepts

tessellations
geometry
slides, flips, turns (transformations)

Materials

grid paper ($\frac{1}{4}$ in. or 1 cm)
colored markers or pencils

Background: The Navajo People

The Navajo were a nomadic people, unlike their Pueblo neighbors. Using instructions from ancient legends, they constructed hogans from logs and sticks covered with mud and sod. Being nomads, they had no reason to build permanent homes.

Sheep were the source not only of food but also clothing and trade. The fact that Navajo women were responsible for the sheep and the weaving underscores the importance of women in Navajo life. The Earth was the mother of the Navajo, and they were her children. In legend, Changing Woman, one of the Holy Ones, was the source of life for the Navajo.

As far back as the mid-1800s, diaries and reports written by scouts and trappers describe the beauty of Navajo blankets. These people were also impressed by the tightness of the weave, remarking that water could actually be carried in a Navajo blanket.

Possible Solutions to the Challenge

• A tessellation of each of the Navajo designs is shown opposite. To tessellate, students can cut out a shape from grid paper and trace around it onto another piece of grid paper. Or students can draw tessellations directly onto grid paper.

• Students can alternate colors when coloring in a tessellation. The Navajo did this for clarity and beauty.

• Students should also feel free to use multiple colors within a shape.

Questions

• Which designs were the easiest to tessellate? Which were the hardest?

• How would you describe a slide, flip, and turn to a younger child? (A slide is the movement of a shape along a straight line. A flip is what the shape looks like in a mirror. A turn is the movement of turning, or rotating, a shape around a certain point.)

• What different methods can be used for investigating whether or not a design will tessellate by itself? (Cut the design out of grid paper and trace around it onto another piece of grid paper. Or just draw the shape over and over again on grid paper. Slide, flip, and turn the shape to see if it tessellates.)

Weaving with Spider Woman

NAVAJO BLANKETS

Introduction

"I know each tree and each tree knows me. In that way, for that reason, I can't move anywhere."
Roberta Blackgoat, Navajo weaver, who is resisting a congressional order to move or give up any claims to her land in Arizona (as quoted in the *San Francisco Chronicle,* May 4, 1977)

Hundreds of years ago, the Navajo (or Diné) were nomads in the area that is now New Mexico and Arizona. They believed the Earth was their mother, who gave them life and supported them. They felt as close to the Earth as to a parent.

The Navajo are famous for their beautifully woven

blankets. They began weaving with wool in the late 1600s after the Spanish explorers introduced sheep to the Southwest. Navajo women did the weaving, and girls as young as three years old helped their mothers. Each blanket could take up to a half year to complete. Amazingly, the Navajo women wove their blankets without a plan.

The Navajo explained how they became such talented weavers by telling a legend. Refer to the picture as you read.

Spider Woman and Spider Man, two of the Holy People, gave weaving to the Navajo. Spider Man taught them how to build the loom, and Spider Woman taught them how to weave. The loom was magnificent. The poles were sky and earth cords, and the warp sticks were sun rays. The heddle sticks were rock crystal and sheet lightning. The batten was a sun halo.

The Challenge

Find out which designs from Navajo blankets will tessellate (repeat) by themselves. Then create a Navajo-style blanket on grid paper by tessellating several of the designs.

Extra: Did you slide, flip, or turn the designs on your blanket when you tessellated them?

What You Will Need

grid paper
colored markers or pencils

The Facts About Navajo Designs

Some designs used by the Navajo are shown on page 7.

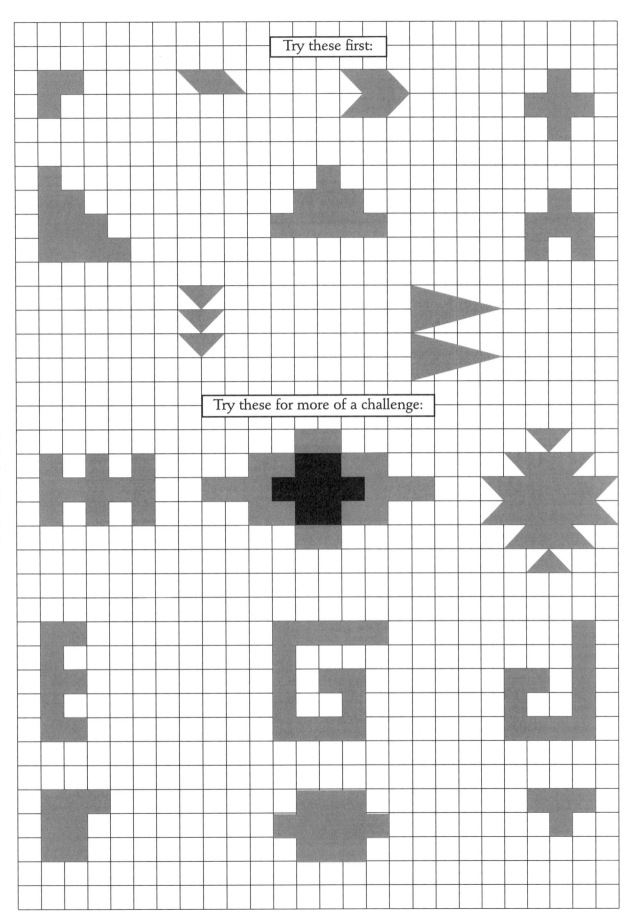

Try these first:

Try these for more of a challenge:

Navajo Blankets 7

The Facts About Tessellations

- To *tessellate* means to cover a surface in all directions using the same shape or shapes. There can be no overlaps and no gaps.

A triangle has been tessellated below:

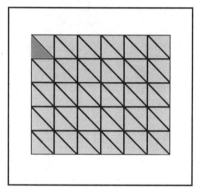

- To figure out how to tessellate a shape, you have to move the shape around by sliding, flipping, or turning it. (Some people use the words translating, reflecting, and rotating instead.)

Slide

If you slide a triangle on a straight line, here's what you get:

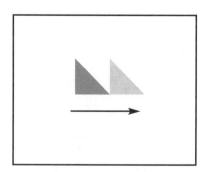

If you keep sliding it, here's what you get:

Flip

If you flip a diamond so that you get its mirror image, here's what you get:

If you keep flipping it, here's what you get:

Turn

If you turn, or rotate, a triangle around, here's what you get:

If you keep turning it, here's what you get:

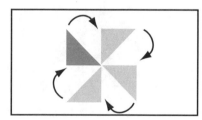

To Do List

- Tessellate each Navajo design shown on page 7. Draw your tessellations on grid paper.
- On another grid paper, make a Navajo-style blanket using at least two of the Navajo designs. On your blanket, tessellate the two designs. Your blanket can also have plain stripes of color.
- Color your blanket using Navajo colors: black, white, yellow, blue, red, green, and brown. (Brown was the natural color of the wool.)

Extra: Write about and show the slides, flips, and/or turns you used to tessellate the designs on your blanket. (These are called *transformations.*)

Example:

Transformations used in the sample blanket:

Start with	Flip	Slide	Slide
Start with	Flip	Turn	

CHAPTER 2
From Triumph to Tragedy

RENÉ-ROBERT CAVALIER, SIEUR DE LA SALLE, FRENCH EXPLORER

From Triumph to Tragedy

RENÉ-ROBERT CAVALIER, SIEUR DE LA SALLE, FRENCH EXPLORER

The Challenge

Students consider what would have happened if the French had settled into colonies on all of the American lands claimed by René-Robert Cavalier, Sieur de La Salle, for France in the late seventeenth century. In fact, La Salle claimed all the "seas, harbors, . . . nations, peoples, provinces, cities, towns, villages, . . . streams, and rivers" that flowed into the Mississippi River. Students estimate how many square miles that would have included, what present-day states or parts of states would have been claimed, and about what fraction of today's United States would have been French. They consider how modern life in the United States might have been different under these circumstances.

Extra: Students figure out how much the Louisiana Purchase cost per square mile.

Math Skills/Concepts

area
fractions
map scale

Materials

ruler
blank map of the United States
scissors (optional)

Background: Archaeologists Find One of La Salle's Sunken Ships

On his last voyage in 1684, La Salle overshot the mouth of the Mississippi River with four ships. One was the *Belle*. La Salle then left the *Belle* in the hands of an inept and drunken pilot while he and a crew set off to explore the wilderness. After the crew of the *Belle* ran out of fresh water, they ran aground trying to sail for land. In 1995 the sunken *Belle* was discovered in the muddy waters off the coast of Texas. Cannons, hundreds of brass rings, and a complete skeleton were among the astounding relics uncovered in the wreck by archaeologists.

Possible Solutions to the Challenge

• Students could outline the area from the Appalachian Mountains to the Rocky Mountains, which is the area drained by the Mississippi and its tributaries. They could cut out a square inch and see how many square inches fit inside the area they outlined. Since they know that 1 inch equals 300 miles on the map, 1 square inch is 90,000 square miles (300 by 300) on the map.

• Or, after outlining the area claimed by La Salle, students might roughly divide it into rectangles and triangles on the map and calculate the area of each. Then they could convert the area to square miles using 1 square inch to equal 90,000 square miles.

• Students may come up with about 900,000 square miles for the area claimed by La Salle. To calculate what fraction of the entire United States that represents, students should find the total number of square miles covered by the United States. It turns out that the area claimed by La Salle covered about half of the continental United States.

• If France had settled the land claimed by La Salle, the French might have taken over all of North America; French might be the main language in the United States; and the colonists might have fought a revolution to gain independence from France. Or, America might have developed more like Europe, with separate countries speaking different languages—English, French, and Spanish.

Extra: The Louisiana Purchase covered 830,000 square miles and cost $15 million. That's about $18 per square mile.

Questions

• How can you use the scale on the map? (Students need to work in miles and square miles. They can use the fact that 1 inch equals 300 miles and so 1 square inch is 90,000 square miles. They could cut a square inch out of paper and use it to find the number of square miles La Salle claimed.)

• The scale is in miles. How can you use it to figure out square miles?

• What information do you need to figure out what fraction of America La Salle claimed for France? (square miles La Salle claimed and square miles in all of the continental United States)

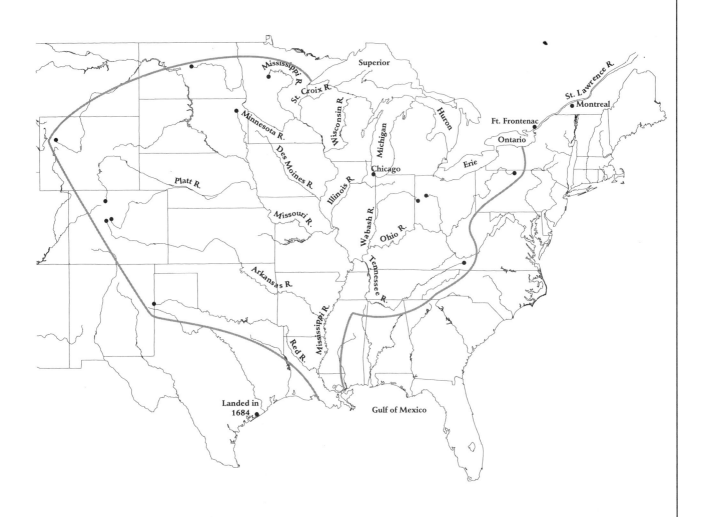

From Triumph to Tragedy

RENÉ-ROBERT CAVALIER, SIEUR DE LA SALLE,

FRENCH EXPLORER

La Salle described one of his journeys:

*". . . we must suffer all the time from hunger; sleep on the open ground, and often without food; watch by night and march by day, loaded with baggage, such as blanket, clothing, kettle, hatchet, gunpowder, lead, and skins to make moccasins; sometimes pushing through thickets, sometimes climbing rocks covered with ice and snow, sometimes wading whole days through marshes where the water was waist-deep, or even more, at a season when the snow was not entirely melted. . . ." ***

Introduction

Personality René-Robert Cavalier, Sieur de La Salle, came to the New World at the age of twenty-three. In 1666 he was well educated, fearless of physical danger, and, as you will see, extraordinarily energetic and determined. He was, however, overly silent, and he harshly ignored others' feelings, often angering his crew members by pushing them beyond reason. La Salle was obsessed with setting up forts along the Mississippi River and claiming all the land around it for France.

Determination

La Salle and his men set out in birchbark canoes many times, with mishaps that would have stopped others. He survived a number of assassination attempts and lost ships loaded with furs and supplies. Deserters destroyed some of the forts he had built. He trekked thousands of miles back and forth to find lost companions, replenish supplies, and calm his debtors. La Salle's friendship with, and respect for, the Native Americans saved his life and the lives of his crew time and time again. He learned eight native languages and always carried a peace pipe.

Triumph Finally, in 1682, after twelve years of attempts, La Salle made it from the St. Lawrence River all the way to the mouth of the Mississippi River. He claimed all the land drained by the Mississippi and its tributaries for France and called it "Louisiana."

* Jim Hargrove, *The World's Great Explorers.* Chicago, IL: Childrens Press, 1990, pp. 82, 98.

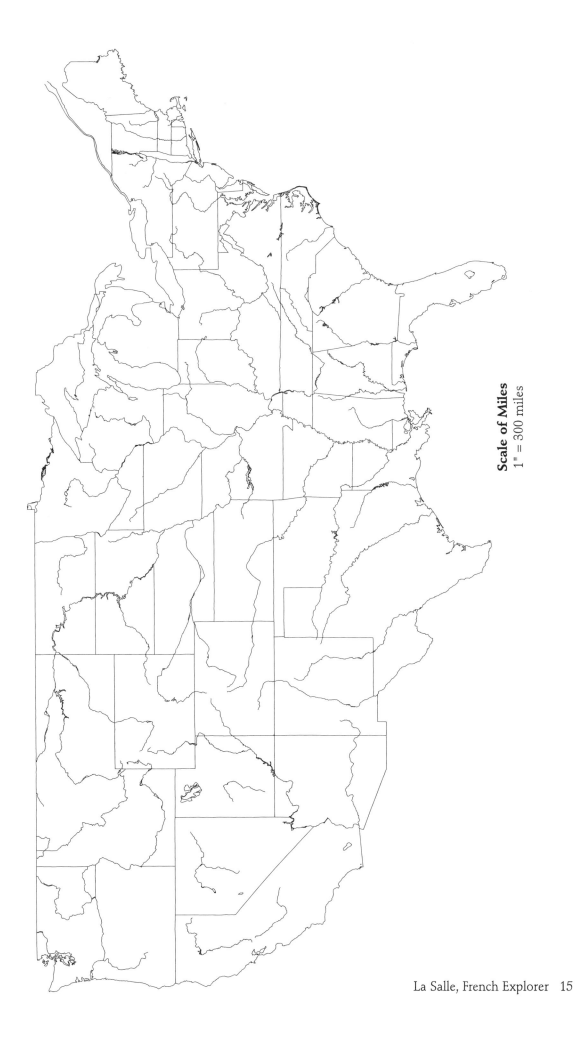

Scale of Miles
1" = 300 miles

- Label these features on the map:
  rivers flowing into the Mississippi River
  St. Lawrence River
  Montreal, Canada
  Great Lakes
  Gulf of Mexico
  approximate spot where La Salle landed in Texas
- Draw a line around the area that La Salle claimed for France.
- Study the scale on the map. How big is a square mile on the map? Figure out a strategy for finding how many square miles La Salle claimed.
- Figure out approximately what fraction of the continental United States he claimed.
- Write about what life in the United States might be like today if the French had settled on the land claimed by La Salle.

Extra: Figure out how much the Louisiana Purchase cost per square mile.

Tragedy After returning to France, he brought back 300 settlers hoping to establish a colony at the mouth of the Mississippi River. But he miscalculated and landed 400 miles west of the river, in present-day Texas! He explored the area, looking for the Mississippi, but never found it again. On his last effort to get help for the sick and starving settlers who remained, his men ambushed him and shot him to death. He was forty-three. France, after all, did end up claiming the land west of the Mississippi. Spain owned it for a time until Napoleon got it back for the French. In 1803 Napoleon sold it to President Thomas Jefferson for $15 million, a transaction known today as the Louisiana Purchase.

The Challenge

What if the French had settled into colonies the way the English did on the east coast of America? Suppose they had done this on all the land claimed by La Salle for France. In fact, La Salle claimed all the "seas, harbors, . . . nations, peoples, provinces, cities, towns, villages, . . . streams, and rivers" that flowed into the Mississippi.* How many square miles would that have included? Which present-day states or parts of states would France have claimed? About what fraction of today's United States would have been French? How would life be different in the United States now?

What You Will Need

ruler
blank map of the United States
scissors (optional)

The Facts

- La Salle claimed all the land around the rivers that drained into the Mississippi.
- On his last voyage, La Salle landed about 400 miles west of the Mississippi, in Texas.
Extra: The Louisiana Purchase included the land west of the Mississippi and east of the Rocky Mountains.

* Jim Hargrove, *The World's Great Explorers*. Chicago, IL: Childrens Press, 1990, pp. 82, 98.

CHAPTER 3

Did Betsy Ross Really Sew It?

THE STARS AND STRIPES

Did Betsy Ross Really Sew It?
THE STARS AND STRIPES

The Challenge

Just like the people who designed each new flag as different states entered the Union, students will be designing flags with different numbers of stars. Before starting, students will write down how many stars they think decorate the classroom flag (without peeking). They will draw a picture of how they think the stars are arranged. Then they will think about the number of stars on various flags throughout history: Is each number prime or composite? What are the factors of the number?

Extra: Students show the number of stars on the flags they design as equations. Then they write about what primes, composites, factors, and equations have to do with flag design.

Math Skills/Concepts

factors
prime and composite numbers
patterns
symmetry
algebra (optional)

Materials

grid paper
scissors
2 square pieces of paper or origami paper (optional)

Background: The Arrangement of Stars on the Flag

Designing American flags has a relevance to history because for a long time there was no prescribed way to arrange the stars. Congress waited until 1912 to make a law describing the official arrangement.

It is interesting to study some of the arrangements of stars on the canton of versions of the Stars and Stripes. Some of the stars are arranged in patterns or in symmetrical designs even though the number of stars is prime (13 or 37 stars, for instance). Likewise, on other flags, the stars form a pattern even though the number of stars is composite with very few factors (33 stars). Surprisingly, the traditional flag with 25 stars was not arranged in five rows of five stars.

Possible Solutions for the Challenge

On the following two pages are the cantons of real flags that have flown throughout U. S. history.

13

13

13

13

13

13

15

20

21

23

24

25

26

27

28

29

30

31

32

33

33

34

34

5

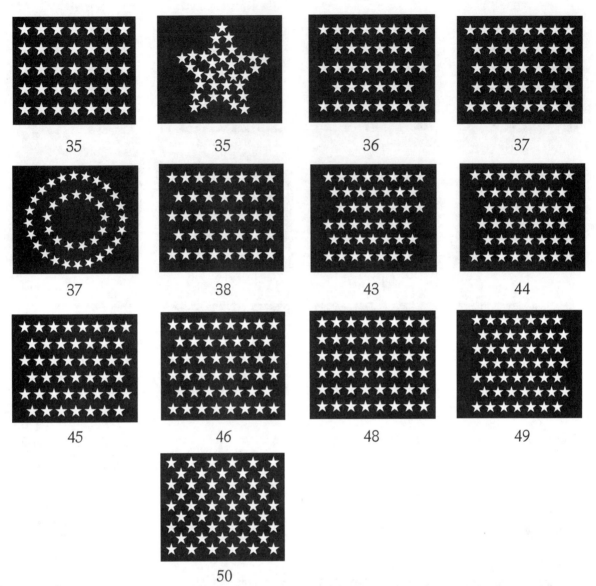

35   35   36   37

37   38   43   44

45   46   48   49

50

Q u e s t i o n s

- Can any prime number of stars be represented in a symmetrical pattern? Which ones? (e.g., 13, 37)
- Can all composite numbers of stars be represented in a symmetrical pattern that would fit into a rectangular canton close to this shape? Explain. (No, some numbers of stars, such as 27, do not fit well into this rectangular shape even though they are composite.)

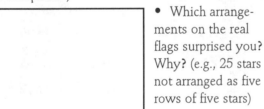

- Which arrangements on the real flags surprised you? Why? (e.g., 25 stars not arranged as five rows of five stars)

Extra: For the flag with 32 stars, a possible equation is $(7 \times 2) + (6 \times 3) = 32$. Equations can help you analyze how a flag in history was arranged in rows. Primes, composites, and factorization have to do with flag design because the number of stars need to be divided into rows. Sometimes these rows can be equal and sometimes symmetrical depending on whether the number (of stars) has many factors, few factors, or no factors.

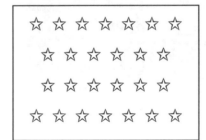

Did Betsy Ross Really Sew It?

THE STARS AND STRIPES

Introduction

It has become popular to question stories in history. Many people question the story of how and by whom the first flag of the United States was designed and sewn. On the right is the story, and on the left, the questions:

The Questions

Why did the grandson wait until he was 45 years old to tell the story?

George Washington was in Pennsylvania in June 1776, but he was busy with the war. Why take time to see a seamstress?

Why have a flag made before the Declaration of Independence?

If the flag was made in June 1776, why did Congress wait until June 1777 to adopt it?

Why aren't there any receipts or notes from a flag committee? There are receipts for flags Betsy Ross made later. (Note that there are no records of any flag committee, even in 1777.)

What do you think? Did Betsy Ross sew the first flag?

The Story

The grandson of Betsy Ross was 11 when his grandmother died at the age of 84, but many times before her death, she had told him the story of sewing the first flag of the United States. In 1870, ninety-four years after the Declaration of Independence was adopted, the grandson of Betsy Ross finally decided to make the story official.

He said that Betsy Ross was a 24-year-old seamstress in Pennsylvania who had done some sewing work for the Washingtons. In June of 1776, one month before the Declaration of Independence was signed, George Washington, Robert Morris, and George Ross (a relative of Betsy Ross) came to call on her. The men showed her Washington's design for the new flag. She suggested that it be rectangular rather than square and that the stars have five points instead of six.

The Challenge

Just like the people who designed each new flag as different states entered the Union, you will be designing flags with different numbers of stars. Before you start, write down how many stars you think are on the flag in your classroom. (Don't peek.) Draw a picture of how you think they are arranged. Then think about the number of stars on various flags throughout history: Is each number prime or composite? What are the factors of each number? *Extra:* Show the number of stars on each flag you design as an equation. What do primes, composites, factors, and equations have to do with flag design?

What You Will Need

grid paper
scissors
2 square pieces of paper, or origami paper (optional)

The Facts

- From 1777 to today, there have been many American flags. The first flag, the one Betsy Ross might have sewn, had 13 stars and 13 stripes. As each state joined the Union, both a star and a stripe were added. In 1818 the stripes were getting too narrow. Congress agreed on 13 stripes and a new star for each state.
- Until 1912, the pattern of the stars on the flag wasn't set. Flag designers could arrange the stars in any way. Some placed the stars in rows, some in circles, some in star formations.
- This chart shows when each star was added to the U. S. flag. Find your state in the list and read through the others.

June 14, 1777	13 stars and 13 stripes for the original states: Delaware, Pennsylvania, New Jersey, Georgia, Connecticut, Massachusetts, Maryland, South Carolina, New Hampshire, Virginia, New York, North Carolina, Rhode Island
1795	15 stars and 15 stripes: Vermont, Kentucky This was the flag when Francis Scott Key wrote the "Star-Spangled Banner." From a British ship on which he was being held, Key saw the flag flying over Ft. McHenry in the morning light of September 14, 1812. The actual flag has 11 bullet holes in it.
1818	20 stars: Tennessee, Ohio, Louisiana, Indiana, Mississippi Congress decided to go back to 13 stripes.
1819	21 stars: Illinois
1820	23 stars: Alabama, Maine
1822	24 stars: Missouri
1836	25 stars: Arkansas
1837	26 stars: Michigan
1845	27 stars: Florida
1846	28 stars: Texas
1847	29 stars: Iowa
1848	30 stars: Wisconsin
1851	31 stars: California

1858	32 stars: Minnesota
1859	33 stars: Oregon
1861	34 stars: Kansas The flag with 34 stars flew over Ft. Sumter in the first battle of the Civil War. The first Confederate flag was made the same year. It was called the Stars and Bars.
1863	35 stars: West Virginia
1865	36 stars: Nevada
1867	37 stars: Nebraska
1877	38 stars: Colorado On June 14, 1877, the first Flag Day was observed. What is significant about that day and year?
1890	43 stars: North Dakota, South Dakota, Montana, Washington, Idaho
1891	44 stars: Wyoming
1892	Pledge of Allegiance written
1896	45 stars: Utah
1908	46 stars: Oklahoma
1912	48 stars: New Mexico, Arizona
1959	49 stars: Alaska
1960	50 stars: Hawaii

To Do List

- Look at all the numbers of stars on the American flag throughout history. Record the prime numbers. For the other numbers of stars, record the factors.
- Choose 10 flags to design. Among your 10 flags, include at least two flags with a prime numbers of stars, a flag with 13 stars, and the flag that was made when your state joined the Union.
- Design only the canton (the star part of the flag) for the 10 flags you chose.
- Design your cantons in symmetrical or organized patterns, if possible.
- Your canton should be a rectangle similar to this one. (Of course, it can be larger.)
- When you are done, ask your teacher to show you pictures of the real flags in American history. Compare them to your designs.

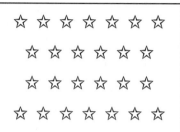
For Fun: According to legend, Betsy Ross suggested to Washington that a five-pointed star could be made in "one snip" of the scissors. Here's one way to do that. Try it. You will need a square paper and scissors.

More fun: A six-pointed star could have been made with one snip as well. Try folding a square paper and cutting it to make a six-pointed star.

1. Fold the paper in half.

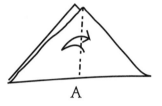

2. Fold the paper in half again and unfold.

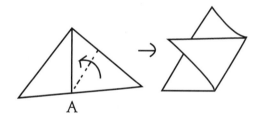

3. Fold as shown.

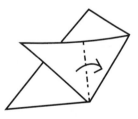

4. Fold the top triangle in half.

Adapted from Kunihiko Kasahara, *Origami Omnibus*. Tokyo: Japan Publications, 1988, p. 75.

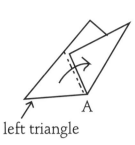

left triangle

5. Fold the left triangle on
   the dotted line.

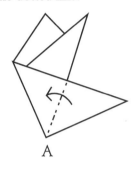

A

6. Fold the top triangle in half.

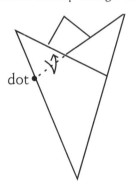

dot •

7. Fold down and unfold.
   Make a dot as shown.

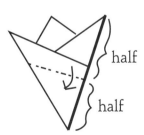

half

half

8. Fold the whole figure down
   by folding the right side of the
   figure in half. (The right side is
   darkened in the drawing.)

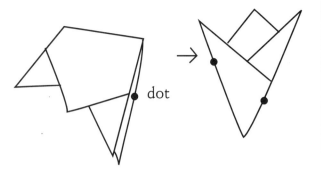

dot

9. Make a dot as shown. Make the
   dot so you'll see it when you
   unfold the figure. Unfold.

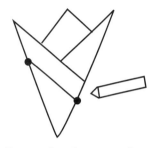

10. Draw a line between the
    two dots.

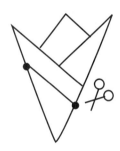

11. Cut along the line.

12. Open up the paper.

Adapted from Kunihiko Kasahara, *Origami Omnibus*. Tokyo: Japan Publications,
1988, p. 75.

CHAPTER 4

Blending African and American Traditions

AFRICAN AMERICAN QUILTERS

Blending African and American Traditions

AFRICAN AMERICAN QUILTERS

The Challenge

Students choose a traditional design from early America, either one of the patterns shown or another with which they are familiar. They then create an African American-inspired quilt design, using all or some of the elements described in the box on page 34. Using friendly fractions (compatible fractions), they figure out approximately what fraction of their quilt is covered by each color. Then they order the friendly fractions.

Extra: Students order the fractions by changing them to decimals or percents. Then students describe the relationships between each color on the quilt using fractions, decimals, or percents.

Math Skills/Concepts

geometry
estimating fractions
equivalent fractions
friendly fractions
comparing and ordering fractions
changing fractions to decimals or percents and
    comparing (optional)

Materials

grid paper
colored markers or pencils

Background: Roland Freeman Meets African American Quilters

Roland L. Freeman, a renowned photodocumentarian, wrote a beautiful book called *A Communion of the Spirits,* in which he spoke with and photographed African American quilters from 38 states and the District of Columbia. As an African American man, he felt his findings were less restrictive than those of researchers who had come before him. He found that African American women and men quilted for a variety of reasons and that some quilts did not fit the generalizations made about African American quilts. For example, some designs were not variations on traditional patterns. Others were clearly symmetrical. The stories he tells about meeting the quilters are very moving. He saw and slept under quilts that had healing powers, quilts that were records of family histories and the history of slavery, quilts that memorialized both struggles and triumphs, quilts that were made for protection, and quilts that were made simply for warmth.

Possible Solutions to the Challenge

- For the design on page 32, students will arrive at the following fractions, which have been converted to friendly fractions:

Light Grey:

$$\frac{40}{180} = \frac{40^{\frac{1}{2}}}{180} \times \frac{2}{2} = \frac{81^{\frac{1}{2}}}{360} \approx \frac{80}{360} = \frac{8}{36} \approx \frac{9}{36}$$

a little less than $\frac{1}{4}$.

Dark Grey:

$$\frac{19^{\frac{1}{2}}}{180} = \frac{39}{360} \approx \frac{40}{360}$$

a little less than $\frac{1}{9}$.

Black: $\frac{20}{180} = \frac{1}{9}$ **White:** $\frac{100}{180} = \frac{5}{9}$

- The fractions are shown in order here from largest to smallest:

    White: $\frac{5}{9}$

    Light Grey: a little less than $\frac{1}{4}$

    Black: $\frac{1}{9}$

    Dark Grey: a little less than $\frac{1}{9}$

In this case, comparisons can be made by just looking at the fractions. For other quilts, comparisons can be made by changing all fractions to a common denominator.

Extra: Students can also compare the fractions by dividing the numerators of the fractions by the denominators to change the fractions to decimals or percents. Students can then describe the relationship between colors on their quilts, using fractions, decimals, or percents. For example, in this case, dark grey cover $\frac{39}{360}$ or about $\frac{1}{9}$ of the quilt. This is about 11% of the quilt. White covers $\frac{5}{9}$ of the quilt, or about 56%. The quilt has approximately five times as much white as dark grey.

Questions

- Explain the different ways that the quilt on page 32 was made asymmetrical. (The colors aren't symmetrical; one design is "inside out"; and the

design in the upper right has a different shape on the bottom.)
- A fraction involves a part and a whole. If you are figuring out what fraction of your quilt design is red, what is the whole? How would you express it in numbers? (The quilt on page 32 has a total of 180 squares in the whole design.)
- What can you do with a fraction like: $\frac{40^{\frac{1}{2}}}{144}$

$$\frac{40^{\frac{1}{2}}}{144} = \frac{40^{\frac{1}{2}}}{144} \times \frac{2}{2} = \frac{81}{288}$$

You could multiply the numerator and denominator by 2 to get rid of the fraction in the numerator.

- What strategies can you use to find friendly fractions? (Reduce the fraction. Or find a number close to the numerator that is a factor of the denominator. Or find a number close to the denominator that is a multiple of the numerator. Or change both the numerator and denominator to "neighboring" numbers that allow you to reduce.)
- What do you have to do to order fractions? (Change them to a common denominator.)

Extra:
- What other methods can you use to order fractions? (Change them to decimals or percents by dividing the numerator by the denominator.)
- Suppose $\frac{1}{5}$ (20%) of the design is light grey and $\frac{3}{5}$ (60%) is black. What could you say about the relationship between light grey and black? (There is three times as much black.) What can you say about the relationship between colors on your quilt?

Blending African and American Traditions

AFRICAN AMERICAN QUILTERS

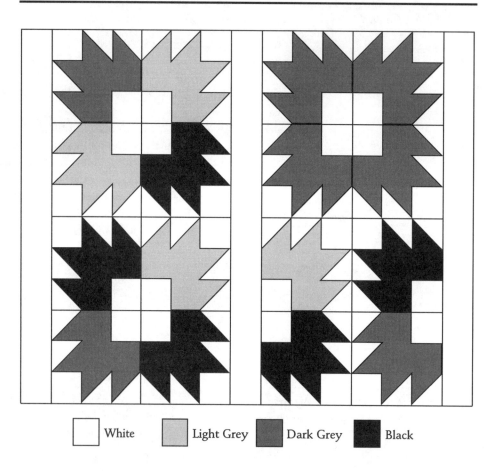

☐ White   ▨ Light Grey   ▨ Dark Grey   ■ Black

Introduction

Among Africans shipped to the southern colonies as slaves, quilting was one way to keep African and family traditions alive. Laws otherwise forbade slaves from practicing their own religions and honoring their spiritual beliefs. Many of the quilts that the African women made for their families looked as if they were influenced by designs from their motherland, Africa. Although the African women used many of the early American quilt patterns—stars, the log cabin, the bear claw—the quilts had a special look and feeling to them.

Of course, each quilt and quilter is unique, but people have noticed that since colonial times, certain elements frequently appear in African American quilts:

• Many quilts use bright, bold, contrasting colors.
• The designs are often large.
• The quilts often have long strips or bands of color between the quilt patterns. (Men in West Africa weave in long strips and sew the strips together. Is there a connection?)
• The designs on the quilts are often asymmetrical (not symmetrical). (Africans

believed that asymmetrical designs kept away evil spirits that traveled in straight lines. Is there a connection?)

• Many quiltmakers repeated an early American pattern over and over but each time changed it in some way.

For twenty years, African American photographer Roland L. Freeman traveled around the United States meeting and photographing African American quilters. He found that many quilts fit the description above and many didn't. The African American quilters Freeman met quilted for many reasons, but some of the quilts he photographed were powerful records of family history and American history. Some quilters he talked to said they were inspired by their ancestors, who sometimes appeared to them in dreams. Other women and men had old quilts or pieces of old quilts. Some said they had sewed a piece of an ancestor's clothing into a new quilt to record family history or to keep a memory alive.

The Challenge

Choose a traditional early American design, either one of the patterns shown here or another with which you are familiar. Create an African American–inspired quilt design, using all or some of the elements shown below. Using friendly fractions, figure out approximately what fraction of your quilt each color covers. Then order the friendly fractions.

Extra: Order the fractions by changing them to decimals or percents. Then describe the relationships between the colors on your quilt, using fractions, decimals, or percents.

What You Will Need

grid paper
colored markers or pencils

The Facts

Here are some common early American quilt patterns.

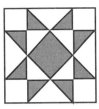

Evening Star

LeMoyne Star

Shoofly

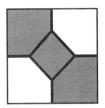

Bowtie

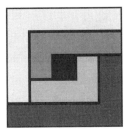

Log Cabin

Goose in the Pond

Courthouse Steps

To Do List

- Choose a quilt pattern from early America. The pattern should include more than just squares in its design.
- Repeat the pattern over and over on grid paper. Your completed design should cover at least an 8-square by 8-square grid.
- Color in the design, keeping in mind the characteristics of many African American quilts. Use bright colors that contrast with each other.
- Make your design asymmetrical by:
  1. using a pattern over and over, but coloring each repetition differently;
  2. varying the size of the pattern when you repeat it;
  3. not lining up the patterns exactly side by side or under one another; or
  4. changing the shapes in the pattern slightly, turning the pattern sideways, or turning the pattern "inside out."

  Look at the design at the beginning of the project. What has been done to make it asymmetrical?
- List the colors in your quilt. Estimate what fraction of your whole quilt design is covered by each color you used. Then find the real fractions. Write about your strategy for finding the fractions.
- Change each fraction you got to a friendly fraction.
- Take the friendly fractions you found for each color and put them in order from largest to smallest. Be sure you know which fraction goes with which color.

Extra:
- Change the original fractions or the friendly fractions to decimals or percents and then put them in order from largest to smallest.
- Use your fractions, decimals, or percents to write about the relationships between the colors on your quilt.

Example: "Light grey covers a little less than $\frac{1}{2}$ or 49%, of the quilt I designed. It is the color I used the most. Black covers about $\frac{1}{4}$ of the quilt, or 23%. There is about twice as much light grey as black."

Some friendly fractions are listed here.

$\frac{1}{2}, \frac{1}{3}, \frac{1}{4}, \frac{1}{5}, \frac{1}{6}, \frac{1}{7}, \frac{1}{8},$

$\frac{2}{3}, \frac{3}{4}, \frac{2}{5}, \frac{3}{5}, \frac{4}{5}, \frac{5}{6},$

$\frac{2}{7}, \frac{3}{7}, \frac{4}{7}, \frac{5}{7}, \frac{6}{7},$

$\frac{3}{8}, \frac{5}{8}, \frac{7}{8}$

Examples of Changing to Friendly Fractions:

$\frac{15}{28}$ is about $\frac{14}{28}$ or $\frac{1}{2}$.

$\frac{3}{17}$ is about $\frac{3}{18}$, or $\frac{1}{6}$.

$\frac{78}{119}$ is about $\frac{80}{120}$ or $\frac{2}{3}$.

$\frac{44}{84}, = \frac{11}{21}$, which is about $\frac{11}{22}$, or $\frac{1}{2}$.

CHAPTER 5
Sheepes Tongue Pie

A SELECTION OF COLONIAL RECIPES

Sheepes Tongue Pie
A SELECTION OF COLONIAL RECIPES

The Challenge

Students figure out the ingredients they would need if they prepared a colonial meal to serve everyone in the class. To do this, they refer to colonial recipes for a breakfast dish and a complete dinner menu. Many of the recipes, such as Breakfast Scrapple made with pig's feet, are obviously not for cooking in the classroom. You may decide to have the class cook some of the simpler recipes, such as Boston Brown Bread, Apees (cookies), Peanut Chews, or Hot Molasses Cider.

Extra: Students refer to the recipes to answer questions involving fractions.

Math Skills/Concepts
adding fractions
multiplying fractions

Materials
ingredients for Peanut Chews, Boston Brown Bread, Apees, or Hot Molasses Cider (optional)

Background: Explanation of Recipes on Student Pages
Scrapple is a breakfast food that is chilled in a pan, sliced, and fried. It has a great taste, but an unappealing gray color. For the meat dish, turkey slices are added to a creamy oyster sauce and warmed. For the vegetable dish, layers of beans and corn are topped with tomato, sugar, and seasonings, and then with cheese. Boston Brown Bread used to be steamed in a kettle in the fireplace. Apees were first thought of as cakes, rather than cookies. You might want to have your class make one of the simple recipes, such as Boston Brown Bread or Apees. Or

they could prepare one of the recipes on the top of page 37, which require only a hot plate. Students will have to alter the recipes to fit the class size.

Possible Solutions to the Challenge
• To adjust recipes to feed the class, students can use a number of strategies. Suppose that there are 30 students in the class:
1. The scrapple recipe serves four. Multiply the ingredients for scrapple by 8 since 8 x 4 = 32 and 32 is close to 30.
2. The recipe for Boston Brown Bread makes 20 slices. The class needs 10 more slices. They would need the original ingredients plus half again (or $1\frac{1}{2}$ times the original ingredients). For example, they would need $\frac{3}{4}$ c + $\frac{3}{8}$ c = $1\frac{1}{8}$ c cornmeal.
• When students consolidate the ingredients that are repeated in more than one recipe, they will need to find totals for cornmeal, sugar, salt, margarine or butter, flour, pepper, and eggs.

Peanut Chews
serves 30–35

$\frac{1}{2}$ cup honey

$\frac{3}{4}$ cup maple syrup

$\frac{1}{4}$ teaspoon baking soda

$\frac{1}{4}$ teaspoon cream of tartar

1 cup roasted peanuts

Heat honey and maple syrup in a saucepan. Wait about 10–15 minutes until a small portion becomes a hard ball when dropped into very cold water. (Be careful. It's very sticky at this point.) Remove mixture from heat. Mix in soda and cream of tartar and nuts. Pour into a greased 8 x 8 x 2 inch pan. Cool. Cut into about 64 one-inch squares.

Hot Molasses Cider
serves 6

6 whole cloves

2 lemon slices

4 cups apple cider or apple juice

$\frac{1}{4}$ cup molasses

1 cinnamon stick

Juice of 1 lemon

Stick cloves in lemon slices. Add all ingredients except lemon juice and bring to a boil. Simmer 10 minutes. Mix in lemon juice.

Extra:

• To answer the question about the broth in the original Breakfast Scrapple recipe, students will have to multiply the amount of cornmeal ($\frac{3}{4}$ cup) by 3 to get $2\frac{1}{4}$ cups of broth.

• When students halve the amount of raisins in the original bread recipe, they will get $\frac{3}{8}$ cup. One solution is to fill the measuring cup that holds $\frac{1}{4}$ cup only halfway. This can be done three times to measure out $\frac{3}{8}$ cup raisins.

• To measure $\frac{2}{3}$ cup sour cream with measuring cups that hold $\frac{1}{2}$ and $\frac{1}{4}$, one solution is to find a quantity between $\frac{1}{2}$ and $\frac{1}{4}$ cup.

Questions

• How many students are in your class? If you want to adjust recipes to your class size, what strategy can you use for recipes that feed four or six people? (See possible solutions.)

• What strategy can you use to adjust recipes that feed 20 people? (See possible solutions.)

• When adjusting recipes, can you multiply in your head or do you need pencil and paper?

• What are some shortcuts and methods for multiplying a whole number by a fraction or mixed number? (You can change the mixed number to an improper fraction before multiplying. You can cancel out common factors. Or you can multiply the whole number times each part of the mixed number and add.)

• How can you add ingredients with different denominators? (Change to a common denominator.)

• After doubling or tripling recipes, what do you need to do with improper fractions; that is, fractions in which the numerator is larger than the denominator? Why? (You need to change to mixed numbers to use standard measuring spoons and cups.)

• What are some of the main ingredients in colonial recipes? (meat, corn, flour, sugar or molasses, cornmeal, salt, cream or milk) What does this tell you about those times? (Corn was plentiful. They probably raised and ate their own animals for meat. They didn't realize the health effects of eating a lot of sugar, salt, and rich creams.)

Sheepes Tongue Pie

A SELECTION OF COLONIAL RECIPES

To make a sheepes tongue pie: Boyle ye tongues tender, then pill them and slit ym in ye middle and lay them in ye pie, like an oyster pie, with sum butter grated bread, & nutmegg, & some salt; and when it is baked, melt and beat some butter and white wine together, and some capers which have been scallded in water, & as much sugar as you please. then cut ye lid open, and poure it all in, & then serve it up, without setting it into the oven againe.*

Introduction

Colonial recipes give you a peek into daily life in the American colonies. But be forewarned! The women, who did the cooking, were not health conscious in the same ways we are today. They thought nothing of dumping a pound of butter into what they were cooking or using "as much sugar as you please" (if they were wealthy enough to have butter and sugar, that is). In fact, they used so much sugar, molasses, and honey that many people lost their teeth early in life. Cholesterol was obviously not an issue either, considering all the rich cream and eggs the recipes called for.

Strange Recipe Names

Even the names of recipes are entertaining: How to Souse a Pigg of 3 or 4 shillings price; How to boyle pigeons Wth puddings; How to make pease porrage of old pease; How to stew an eele; How to pickle clove gilleflowers and other flowers. There were also Apple crowdy, Mess apple pies, and Fooles (pureed fruit mixed with custard).

Typical American Foods

Some foods originated in the Americas and were used by natives of North, Central, and South America. You might have guessed that turkey and corn are on that list. (Ben Franklin wanted the turkey to be the national symbol instead of the bald eagle.) But what about kidney beans, white and sweet potatoes, tomatoes, and pineapples (a favorite of Thomas Jefferson)?

*From Karen Hess, transcriber, *Martha Washington's Booke of Cookery.* New York, NY: Columbia University Press, 1981, p. 90.

Chocolate and vanilla are also native American ingredients.

How the Native Americans Helped

Without the Native Americans, the colonists wouldn't have known how to bake beans or how to keep meat by drying, salting, or pickling it. That's how beef jerky came about. Of course, the Native Americans taught their neighbors how to fertilize corn by burying a fish in the hole with the seeds. Colonial children even learned to pop popcorn in the fireplace. Pumpkins were also a Native American food that the colonists used in various ways, including as pie filling. Pies with the top crust were called "coffins" and those with only a bottom crust were called "traps."

Mind Your Manners

Good manners for children included wiping or licking dirty fingers, not licking the plate, not putting back food already taken, and not throwing bones under the table or tablecloth. Men and older boys were allowed to wear their hats at the table.

The Challenge

Figure out the ingredients you would need if you prepared a colonial meal to serve everyone in your class. To do this, refer to the colonial recipes here, which include a breakfast dish and a complete dinner menu. Many of the recipes, such as Breakfast Scrapple made with pig's feet, are obviously not for cooking in the classroom. You may be able to cook some of the simpler recipes, such as Boston Brown Bread, Apees (cookies), Peanut Chews, or Hot Molasses Cider. (Your teacher can provide the last two recipes.)

Extra: Answer questions involving fractions in the recipes.

What You Will Need

ingredients for Peanut Chews, Boston Brown Bread, Apees, or Hot Molasses Cider (optional)

The Facts

Creamed Turkey and Oysters
serves 4

$\frac{3}{4}$ cup water

3 cups oysters

$\frac{1}{3}$ cup butter or margarine

$\frac{1}{2}$ cup flour

$1\frac{1}{2}$ cups cream

$1\frac{1}{2}$ teaspoons salt

$\frac{1}{2}$ teaspoon pepper

12 slices of turkey

Breakfast Scrapple
serves 4

4 pig's feet

2 pounds pork shoulder, bone-in

Pig's head, optional

1 pound pork liver

1 teaspoon salt

$1\frac{1}{2}$ cups cornmeal

$\frac{1}{2}$ cup onions, chopped

After making a broth from the meat, you need to add cornmeal. You'll need three times as much broth as cornmeal.

Boston Brown Bread
makes 20 slices

2 tablespoons butter or margarine

$\frac{1}{4}$ cup sugar

1 egg

$\frac{3}{4}$ cup molasses

$2\frac{1}{4}$ cups whole wheat flour

1 teaspoon salt

$\frac{3}{4}$ cup cornmeal

$1\frac{1}{2}$ teaspoons baking powder

$1\frac{1}{2}$ teaspoons baking soda

$1\frac{3}{4}$ cups buttermilk

$\frac{3}{4}$ cup raisins

In bowl 1, mix shortening and sugar. Sift dry ingredients. In bowl 2, beat egg in with molasses and mix in buttermilk and raisins. Mix everything together. Fill two bread pans halfway. Place bread pans in a pan of boiling water and cover with tinfoil. Let steam for 2 to $2\frac{1}{2}$ hours in oven at 275°.

Tomato-Cheese Soybeans
serves 6

1 cup dried soybeans

2 cups cooked kernel corn

$2\frac{1}{3}$ cups tomatoes

1 teaspoon sugar

1 teaspoon seasoned salt

$\frac{1}{8}$ teaspoon pepper

1 cup buttered soft bread crumbs

$\frac{1}{2}$ cup grated Cheddar cheese

paprika

Apees (cookies)
serves 20

$\frac{1}{2}$ cup butter or margarine

$\frac{1}{2}$ teaspoon vanilla

$\frac{3}{4}$ cup sugar

1 egg

$1\frac{1}{8}$ cups flour sifted

$\frac{1}{8}$ teaspoon cream of tartar

$\frac{1}{8}$ teaspoon salt

$\frac{1}{3}$ cup sour cream

In bowl 1, mix margarine and vanilla, and gradually add sugar and eggs. In bowl 2, sift flour, salt, and tartar. Slowly add contents of bowl 2 and sour cream to bowl 1, stirring in one and then the other. Drop teaspoonfuls onto a greased cookie sheet. Bake for 10 minutes at 350°. Cookies are light in color.

To Do List

- Look over the ingredients.
- For each recipe, calculate how much of each ingredient is needed to serve your class.
- Check for ingredients that are used in more than one recipe. Calculate how much of that ingredient is needed altogether for feeding your class. For example, cornmeal appears in two recipes. You need to figure out the total amount of cornmeal needed to feed your class.
- (optional) Make Boston Brown Bread, Apees, Peanut Chews, or Hot Molasses Cider for your class. Before cooking, change the amount of each ingredient to fit your class size.

Extra:

Scrapple: After making a broth from water and pig's feet, you need to put cornmeal in the broth. You need three times as much broth as cornmeal. How many cups of broth would you need for four students?

Boston Brown Bread: Suppose you decided to use half the raisins called for in the recipe that makes 20 slices. What quantity of raisins would that be? How could you measure the raisins if you only had measuring cups for $\frac{1}{2}$ cup and $\frac{1}{4}$ cup?

Apees: How could you measure the sour cream (in the recipe for 20 students) if you only had measuring cups for $\frac{1}{2}$ cup and $\frac{1}{4}$ cup?

CHAPTER 6

"Boston Harbor a teapot tonight!"

THE BOSTON TEA PARTY

"Boston Harbor a teapot tonight!"
THE BOSTON TEA PARTY

The Challenge

Students get a sense of how big a "party" the Boston Tea Party really was. They use facts about the event to figure out how many pounds of tea were destroyed. Then they calculate how much floor space 342 chests of East India tea would take up in the classroom.

Extra: Students compare the volume and weight of the tea to something they're more familiar with—cereal.

Math Skills/Concepts

measurement: length, weight, area, volume
multiplication and division of large numbers

Materials

ruler
calculator
cereal box

Background: Details of the Boston Tea Party

On the night of December 6, 1773, a group of Boston men between the ages of 14 and 58 (most of the younger men were apprentices) covered their heads with hoods and their faces with soot, grease, and cork. No records indicate that they donned feathers, but most artwork depicting the event shows otherwise. The fact that they dressed as "Indians" gives insight into their perception of Native Americans.

So disguised, the patriots proceeded to Griffin's Wharf in Boston Harbor. Working by lantern and torch light, between six and nine o'clock they pitched 342 chests of East India tea into the sea from the decks of British tea ships. The most

famous men on the lists of participants (compiled more than 50 years later) were Paul Revere and Dr. Thomas Young, John Adams's friend and doctor. Some patriots planned to come ahead of time, and others joined the "party" on the spur of the moment.

The job was made harder because the chests were heavy, weighing as much as 400 pounds in some cases, and hard to open with an ax because of a canvas covering. The harbor was at low tide, about two feet deep, which meant that the dumped chests began to stack up. One pile even toppled back onto the deck. Except for one broken padlock that someone fixed anonymously the next morning, no damage was done to the ships. Before leaving the ships, participants carefully emptied the tea from their shoes.

Historians say that the Boston Tea Party and England's response unified the radical and moderate colonists and led to the first Continental Congress and the Revolutionary War.

Possible Solutions to the Challenge

- Patriots dumped about 114 chests of tea per hour.
- To find how many pounds of tea were destroyed, students could:

1. Find the volume of a small container of loose tea:

   2 in. x 4 in. x 1 in. = 8 cu in.

2. Find the volume of a chest of East India tea:

   24 in. x 24 in. x 30 in. = 17,280 cu in.

3. Divide to find out how many small containers would fit inside a chest:

   17,280 cu in. ÷ 8 cu in. = 2,160 small containers fit in a chest

4. Multiply to find how many ounces of tea in a chest:

   2,160 containers x 2 oz = 4,320 oz or 270 lb of tea in a chest

5. Multiply to find how many pounds of tea in all:

   342 chests x 270 lb = 92,340 lb of tea (or 46 tons of tea)

- To find out how much of the classroom floor space would be taken up by the chests at the Tea Party, students could:

1. Find the area of the classroom floor: Suppose the classroom measures 25 ft by 30 ft. Then:

   25 ft x 30 ft = 750 sq ft

2. Find the area taken up by 342 chests with bottoms measuring

   24 in. x 24 in. or 2 ft x 2 ft: 2 ft x 2 ft = 4 sq ft; 4 sq ft x 342 chests = 1,368 sq ft

3. Find how many layers of chests would have to be stacked on the classroom floor: Since

   750 sq ft x 2 = 1,400 sq ft,

there would be about two layers of chests in the classroom.

4. This could also be done by drawing a picture of the classroom on grid paper, with each square representing 1 square foot.

Extra: To compare tea to cereal in terms of volume, students could use a real cereal box to find out how many such boxes add up to a volume of 17,280 cubic inches, the volume of the 342 chests of tea.

1. Find the volume of the cereal box. Suppose the cereal box is 12 in. by 14 in. by 2 in. Then its volume is 336 cu in.

2. Divide to find out how many times bigger the chest is than the cereal box:

> 17,280 cu in. ÷ 336 cu in. ≈
> **51 cereal boxes would fit in a chest**

3. Multiply to find out how many cereal boxes would fit in 342 chests:

> **51 cereal boxes × 342 chests =
> 17,442 cereal boxes**

- To compare tea to cereal in terms of weight, students could use a real cereal box to find out how many boxes of cereal weigh the same as 92,340 lb of tea:

1. Change 92,340 lb of tea to ounces:

> **92,340 lb × 16 oz = 1,477,440 oz**

2. Divide to find out how many cereal boxes would equal the weight of the tea. Suppose the cereal in the box weighed 24 oz. Then:

> **1,477,440 oz ÷ 24 oz = 61,560 boxes of
> cereal,**

which would have about the same weight as the dumped tea.

or

1. Change 24 ounces. of cereal to pounds:

> **24 oz ÷ 16 oz = 1.5 lb**

2. Divide to find out how many cereal boxes would equal the weight of the tea:

> **92,340 lb ÷ 1.5 lb = 61,560 boxes
> of cereal**

Questions

- What dimensions are needed to find the volume of a rectangular solid such as a chest? (height, length, width)
- What is the only fact you know about the weight of tea? (8 cu in. weighs about 2 oz)
- How could the volume of the small container of tea help you find the weight of tea in a chest? Would drawing a picture help? (If you calculate how many small containers are in a chest, you can use the weight of the small container to find the weight of tea in a chest.)
- What information do you need to decide how many layers of tea chests would fit in your classroom? (area of 342 chests and area of classroom floor)

Extra:

- What data do you need from the cereal box? (weight, height, length, and width)
- Why is there such a big difference in the number of cereal boxes that would be needed to equal the volume of the tea and the number of boxes that would be needed to equal the weight of the tea? (Cereal is very light and can't be packed compactly the way tea can, so it takes more boxes of cereal to equal the weight of the tea than to equal the volume of the tea.)

"Boston Harbor a teapot tonight!"

THE BOSTON TEA PARTY

Introduction

Read what people who lived around the time of the Boston Tea Party had to say:*

"Keep your hands out of the pockets of the Americans, and they will be obedient subjects."

Colonel Isaac Barre, a member of the English Parliament who sympathized with the colonists on the subject of the tax on tea

"I tell the noble Lord now, if he don't take off the duty, they won't take the tea."

William Dowdeswell, a member of the English Parliament, warning Lord North, prime minister of England

"I doubt whether there is a greater Incendiary in the King's dominions or a man of greater malignity of heart, or who less scruples any measure ever so criminal to accomplish his purpose. . . ."

Thomas Hutchinson, royal governor of Massachusetts, speaking of the patriot, Samuel Adams, leader of the Sons of Liberty

". . . that fiend Hutchinson. . . ."

Samuel Adams, one of the main instigators of the Boston Tea Party, describing Hutchinson, royal governor of Massachusetts

* Wesley S. Griswold, *The Night the Revolution Began.* Brattleboro, VT: The Stephen Greene Press, 1972, pp. 6, 8, 30.

"This meeting can do nothing more to save the country."
Samuel Adams, speaking at Old South Meeting House on December 16, 1773, after the English refused to return the *Dartmouth,* one of the ships filled with tea, to England

"Boston Harbor a teapot tonight!"
A member of the meeting at Old South Meeting House, shouting after Samuel Adams spoke

"Everything was as light as day, by the means of lamps and torches; a pin might be seen lying on the wharf. I went on board where they were at work, and took hold with my own hands. . . . The chests were drawn up by a tackle—one man bringing them forward [in the hold], another putting a rope around them, and others hoisting them to the deck and carrying them to the vessel's side. The chests were then opened, the tea emptied over the side, and the chests thrown overboard. . . . Although there were many people on the wharf, entire silence prevailed—no clamor, no talking. Nothing was meddled with but the teas on board."
Robert Sessions, a patriot who volunteered on the spur of the moment on the night of the Boston Tea Party, writing when he was an old man

"I never worked harder in my life."
Joshua Wyeth, one of the participants in the Tea Party

"The die is cast. The people have passed the river and cut away the bridge. . . . This is the grandest event which has ever yet happened since the controversy with Britain opened. The sublimity of it charms me!"
John Adams, on December 17, 1773, after the Tea Party

"Adams never was in greater glory."
Governor Hutchinson, writing sarcastically of Samuel Adams

"It is a great folly, which I fear the people will resist to the death, and soon."
General Thomas Gage, Hutchinson's replacement for royal governor of Massachusetts, in response to the restrictions put on Boston after the Tea Party, such as the closing of Boston Harbor, the end of town meetings, and the quartering of soldiers in colonial homes

"The cause of Boston is the cause of America."
George Washington, encouraging other colonies to send food and money to Boston after its port was closed

"Madam, is it lawful for a weary traveler to refresh himself with a dish of tea, provided it has been honestly smuggled or paid no duties?"

"No sir, we have renounced all tea in this place, but I'll make you coffee."
John Adams, asking for tea at Mrs. Huston's tavern in July 1774 when tea was being boycotted; Adams told his wife he had to wean himself from tea and did so.

Washington quote: Alfred F. Young and Terry J. Fife with Mary E. Janzen, *We the People.* Philadelphia: Temple University Press, 1993. *Gage quote:* Alistair Cooke, *Alistair Cooke's America.* New York, NY: Alfred A. Knopf, 1973, p. 105. *Adams/Huston quote:* Paul F. Boller, Jr., *Presidential Anecdotes.* New York, NY: Oxford University Press, 1981, p. 28. *Remaining quotes:* Wesley S. Griswold, *The Night the Revolution Began.* Brattleboro, VT: The Stephen Greene Press, 1972, pp. 92, 99, 104, 108, 109.

The Challenge

Get a sense of how big a "party" the Boston Tea Party really was. Use the facts to figure out how many pounds of tea the patriots destroyed. Then find out how much floor space 342 chests of East India tea would take up in your classroom.

Extra: Compare the volume and weight of the tea to something you're more familiar with—cereal.

What You Will Need

ruler
calculator
empty cereal box (optional)

The Facts

- Patriots dumped 342 chests of East India tea into Boston Harbor.
- The tea was packed very tightly in the chests, making the chests very heavy.
- The size of the chests varied and no records were kept, but a reasonable estimate of their dimensions is 24 in. by 24 in. by 30 in.
- A small container of tea with dimensions of 2 in. by 4 in. by 1 in. weighs about two ounces.
- One pound equals 16 ounces.
- About 110 patriots participated in the Boston Tea Party. (With the help of seven participants, a list was made in 1835. Another list was made in 1884, based on documents passed down by families.)
- The Tea Party took place from 6:00 P.M. to 9:00 P.M.

To Do List

- Find out how many chests were dumped per hour.
- Figure out how many pounds (and/or tons) of tea were involved in the Boston Tea Party. Write about your strategy and show your steps.
- Figure out about how much classroom floor space would be taken up by the 342 chests of East India tea. Would there be more than one layer? Explain.

Extra: Compare the tea to cereal:
1. Find out approximately how many boxes of cereal add up to the volume of tea at the Tea Party.
2. Find out approximately how many boxes of cereal add up to the weight of tea at the Tea Party.

CHAPTER 7

From Licorice to Button Hooks

SHOPPING AT A GENERAL STORE

From Licorice to Button Hooks

SHOPPING AT A GENERAL STORE

The Challenge

Each student has $20 to spend on his or her family at the town's general store. Students imagine that they are living in Vermont in 1827. Using a price list from a general store in the early 1800s, students place orders. Then groups of four or more students combine their orders onto one order sheet.

Extra: Traditional shopkeepers listed prices in English pounds, but customers paid in American dollars. Students create a formula for converting pounds to dollars.

Note: You might want to re-create the goods in a general store and set up shop. Students could simulate buying and selling goods and keep track of sales.

Math Skills/Concepts
adding and multiplying decimals (money)

Materials
price list
calculator (Since calculators didn't exist in 1827, whether or not to allow them is up to you.)

Background: Goods and Remedies from a General Store
The general store in the early 1800s was similar to a mall today. There were goods as varied as shirts, boots, candy, pigs, writing paper, books, and nails. Reading the old ledgers from those times gives an interesting snapshot of the times and the individuals who frequented the general store. Some customers' bills were filled with fabric, thread, and ribbon. Others consisted mainly of tobacco and rum.

The general store was also the place to buy supplies for remedies and cures. The notes of shopkeepers, doctors, and patients give insight into the remedies at the time. Eating sugar with several drops of kerosene was the remedy for a sore throat, while wearing onions around the neck was said to cure a cold. Drinking a solution of cream of tartar and water was prescribed for smallpox. For a boil, a compress of boiled flaxseed was applied.

Possible Solutions to the Challenge
• A sample student order form might look something like this one on p. 53. The math can be done mainly by using mental math.
• The same form can be used when groups of four or more students combine orders. The numbers will be higher, and the math will involve pencil and paper (or calculators, if you want students to use them).

ORDER FORM

Goods	Quantity	Price for one (from price list)	Total cost
chocolate	3 pounds	$0.19 per pound	$0.57
eggs	2 dozen	$0.10 per dozen	$0.20
pigs	2	$1.95	$3.90
apples	3 pounds	$0.08 per pound	$0.24
calico	5 yards	$0.34 per yard	$1.70
shirts	5	$0.75	$3.75
children's shoes	3	$0.38 per pair	$1.14
toothbrush	3	$0.26	$0.78
fine ivory comb	2	$0.19	$0.38
quills	6	$0.04	$0.24
gloves	5	$1.08	$5.40
wool	2 pounds	$0.90	$1.80
		TOTAL	$20.10

Extra: Here are two ways to change from pounds to American dollars:

1. In the facts, students learn that £1.1.3 = $3.55. Students could say that 1 shilling is only about $\frac{1}{20}$ of a pound, so £1.1.3 is about 1 pound. Therefore, 1 pound is about $3.55.

2. In the facts, students learn that £1.10.8 = $5.11. They might reason this way: 8 pence is almost a shilling. So you could say £1.10.8 is almost £1.11.0. Eleven shillings is about half a pound, so £1.11.0 is about $1\frac{1}{2}$ pounds or 1.5 pounds. Since 1.5 pounds = $5.11, they can divide using a calculator. 5.11 ÷ 1.5 = 3.4. So 1 pound is about $3.40.

Questions

- When writing your individual order, will you use mental math or paper and pencil? Explain. (Students will probably use mental math.)
- What strategy did you use to make sure you didn't spend more than $20?
- What is an organized way for your group to combine orders? (One way is to read down the price list, note the total quantity of each item purchased by the group, and multiply the quantity by the price on the price list.)
- When multiplying on the group order form, will you use mental math or pencil and paper? Why? (Students will probably use pencil and paper.)

Extra: What are the only facts you know about the relationship between pounds and American dollars? How can you use these facts? Write about your strategy for changing pounds to American dollars. (See possible solutions.)

From Licorice to Button Hooks

SHOPPING AT A GENERAL STORE

Introduction

The general store in the early 1800s sold everything from licorice to button hooks. There were dolls called "babies," hand-dipped candles, playing cards, charcoal, oats, boots, tonics for the liver, hat feathers, sugar candy, calico (a type of cloth), and more. If you didn't have the money, you could exchange a chicken for goods, or you could shoe the owner's horse for free. When something was bought, the owner would write it up. There were no typewriters or computers then, so handwriting was important. Store owners prided themselves on their fancy script.

Although American money had been minted, some shopkeepers continued to mark their prices in pounds, shillings, and pence. Customers paid in dollars, so the store owners had to be good at mental math, or they had to refer to charts that converted pounds to dollars.

The Challenge

Your family of five lives in Vermont in 1927. Winter is coming, and there are cupboards to stock and clothes to sew. You have $20 to spend at the general store. Use the price list from a general store to place an order. Then combine your order with the other students in your group. Don't forget to buy a treat or two! *Extra:* Create a formula for converting pounds to American dollars.

What You Will Need

price list

The Facts About Shopping at a General Store

This price list shows approximate prices for items in the early 1800s.

Price List

Item	Price
1 toothbrush	
1 diary	$0.26
1 broom	$0.13
1 fine ivory comb	$0.35
1 vial of eye water	$0.19
2 sheets of paper	$0.06
1 quill for quill pen	$0.03
1 penknife	$0.04
1 pint lamp oil	$0.31
1 pr. Beaver gloves	$0.13
1 pr. booties	$1.08
1 pr. children's shoes	$2.25
1 pr. boots	$0.38
1 shirt	$2.54
1 spool thread	$0.75
1 yd ribbon	$0.09
1 yd calico	$0.12
1 yd cotton sheeting	$0.34
1 lb wool	$0.16
silk for bonnet	$0.90
1 lb sugar	$0.88
1 dozen eggs	$0.11
1 lb chocolate	$0.09
1 oz sugar plums	$0.19
1 qt molasses	$0.06
1 pig	$0.12
1 lb apples	$1.95
1 lb almonds	$0.08
	$0.18

To Do List

- Sit in groups of four.
- Each member of your group needs to make a separate order form and order $20 worth of goods from the store. (Don't spend more than $20.) Create an order form something like the one below.
- You will need to order more than one of each item you choose to buy. For example, you need to order more than one yard of calico and more than one pound of almonds.
- When each group member has completed his or her order form, combine your orders with the other members of your group. Complete a group order form (see page 57). Calculators didn't exist in colonial times, so don't use one unless your teacher allows it.

Extra: £1.9.2 means 1 pound, 9 shillings, 2 pence. There are 20 shillings in a pound. There are 12 pence in a shilling.

£1.10.8 = $5.11   £1.1.3 = $3.55

Use the facts about English money (and a calculator, if you wish) to figure out a formula or strategy for changing English pounds/shillings/pence to American dollars.

Order Form

Goods	Quantity (How many?)	Price for one (from price list)	Total cost
chocolate	3 pounds	$0.19 per pound	$0.57

TOTAL $

Group Order Form

Goods	Quantity (How many?)	Price for one (from price list)	Total cost
		TOTAL	$

CHAPTER 8
Wagons Ho!

PACKING A COVERED WAGON

Wagons Ho!
PACKING A COVERED WAGON

The Challenge

Students load a covered wagon and travel from Independence, Missouri, to the Oregon Territory, starting out in May and arriving in October. They make a model of a covered wagon (bed, wheels, and possessions) to scale. Using the model, they decide which items to take, according to the space in the wagon and the weight the oxen can pull.

Extra: Students calculate how many times their wheels will rotate on the journey.

Math Skills/Concepts
measurement: weight, volume, circumference
scale

Materials
1-cm grid paper
tape
scissors

Background: A Child's Life in a Covered Wagon

Much of what we know about pioneer life comes from journals and diaries kept by westbound immigrants. Even children recorded their experiences.

Fun and Pastimes: Playing tag, taking practice shots, and playing with a pet were popular pasttimes for children as they crossed the continent. Books were treasured possessions, including *The Life of Daniel Boone, Pilgrim's Progess,* and *Robinson Crusoe.* Girls spent time on embroidery or quilting. If someone had a violin, music and singing around the campfire made wonderful diversions. One seven-

year-old described a game the boys in his wagon train played with the bloated stomach of a dead ox. He and his friends ran, butted their heads into the stomach, and bounced back. One youngster butted so hard that his head got stuck and he had to be pulled out by the legs.

Chores: Older children tended the livestock, such as cows, mules, oxen, and horses. Children were also responsible for letting the chickens and roosters in and out of the coop and collecting eggs. Boys were allowed to hunt and fish, while girls watched over younger children and the sick. Other duties included collecting dried "buffalo chips" for making fires, fetching fresh water in buckets, and picking berries. Helping with cooking and baking bread (by rolling it out on the wagon seat) were a girl's responsibilities. At night, boys would take turns standing guard.

Hardships: Children wrote about thick dust, fierce storms, and temperatures so cold that inches of ice formed in the buckets. They watched their own family members dying from diseases, accidents, and sometimes starvation. Forging rushing rivers on the wagon bed and pulling wagons up mountain passes were frightening and difficult tasks. Family heirlooms, such as pianos and grandfather clocks, were sometimes tossed from the wagon. Drownings, snakebites, and illness were all too common. The children who made it to the West were changed and strengthened by their journey.

Possible Solutions to the Challenge

Students will make scale models of the covered wagons and belongings. Students will then need to consider the items to bring in terms of weight:
• They may find the following are essential: food, clothing, some sort of bedding, cooking equipment, toolbox, tools, tar bucket, barrels for storing food and carrying water in the desert, extra wagon wheels, extra axle, and extra tongue.
• When adding up the weights of items, they will have to remember to multiply the weight of some items (bedding, clothing) by the number in their party. The weights of barrels, chests, and extra wheels will also need to be multiplied by the quantities taken, since more than one will be necessary.
• Students will have to add in the weight of the people riding in the wagon. They'll need to decide if all three people will ever be in the wagon at once.

Students will need to consider the items to bring in terms of volume.
• They may decide that the essentials (listed above) take up most of the wagon. Students may be able to fit in a few extra items, but they will want to leave room for a sick or tired person to rest in the back. Carrying some items on the outside of the wagon creates more space.
• For students who want to find the volume (*V*) of items:

For rectangular solids:

$$V = \text{length} \times \text{width} \times \text{height}$$

For cylindrical objects:

$$V = \text{area of the base} \times \text{height, where area of the base} = \pi r^2$$

Extra: For calculating how many times the back wheel would rotate, students can find the circumference of a wheel with a 5-foot diameter:

1. $C = 2\pi r$
2. $C = 2 \times 3.14 \times 2.5 = 15.7$ ft
3. 2,000 miles $\times$ 5,280 ft per mile = 10,560,000 ft
4. 10,560,000 $\div$ 15.7 = 672,611 rotations

When using grid paper to make the model of the wagon bed, wheels, and belongings, 1 cm = 1 ft. Here is a pattern for a chest that is 36" by 24" by 18" or 3' by 2' by 11/2':

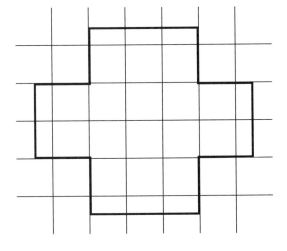

When making scale models, students can either make every item a rectangular solid, or they can make the tublike items by cutting out a circular bottom and wrapping the sides around it.

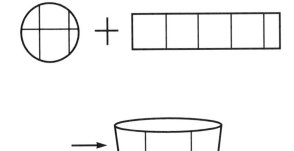

Questions

- What is your strategy for deciding which items to bring in order to keep within the weight limit? (Students may add up the weight of essential items and the weight of people riding in the wagon.)
- What is your strategy for deciding which items will fit in the wagon? (Students may create scale models.)
- How much weight are you allowing for people riding in the wagon? (If someone is sick, three people may be riding in the wagon at once.)
- Which items do you need more than one of? (bedding, clothes, extra wheels, chests, barrels)
- Which imposes more limitations, the weight the oxen can pull or the volume of the wagon bed? Explain. (Students may find that the volume is more restrictive.)
- How do you deal with fractions of a foot when making a scale model? (Most of the fractions are $\frac{1}{2}$ foot, so students can use a half of a square on the grid paper.)

Extra: What information do you need to determine how many times the back wheel will rotate on the journey? (diameter or radius of wheel, circumference of wheel, length of journey)

Wagons Ho!

PACKING A COVERED WAGON

Introduction

Consider these excerpts from pioneer travelers' diaries.*

"When we stopped to make camp, it was pouring rain. . . . For two hours it hailed and rained and blew a perfect gale. When it slacked up a little we got out the provision box and ate a cold supper. Then each one rolled up in a wet blanket and slept until morning."
Eliza McAuley, age 17

". . . As we were just getting up the bank from the ford, our team broke loose and wagon and team backed into the river. . . . I remember the water came rushing into the wagon box to my waist, compelling me to scramble up on the top of a trunk. . . But several men came swimming, held up the wagon, and soon assisted us to the shore."
Jesse A. Applegate, age 7

". . . we had a great fear of Indians but we never saw one until we reached Pacific Springs. Here an old Indian with two squaws and a couple of papooses rode up and traveled with us some miles. This rather took the fear of Indians away."
Mormon diary

". . . On arising next morning we found our oxen mired in the mud, it having rained during the night. We got ropes and pulled out all those we could but I remember our poor old Jerry sinking until nothing could be seen but his nose and we had to leave him to die."
Mormon diary

* *McAuley and Applegate quotes:* Emmy F. Werner, *Pioneer Children on the Journey West.* Boulder, CO: Westview Press, 1995, pp. 11, 115. *Mormon diary excerpts: Book of Remembrance* by the Noyes Family. Reprinted by permission of Lorraine Bates Noyes.

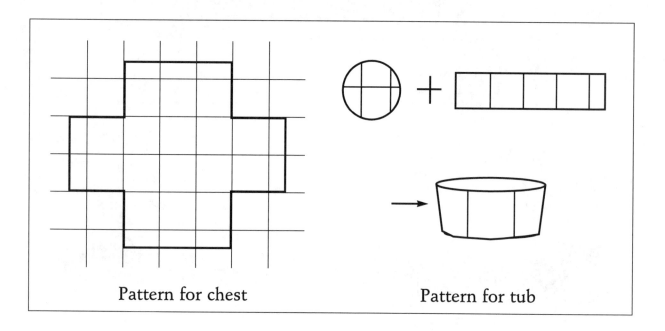

Pattern for chest   Pattern for tub

The Challenge

You and two other class-mates will load a covered wagon and travel from Independence, Missouri, to the Oregon Territory, starting out in May and arriving in October. You will need to make a model of a covered wagon (bed, wheels, and possessions) to scale. Using your model, you will decide which items to take, according to the space in the wagon and the weight the oxen can pull.

Extra: Calculate how many times your back wheels will rotate on the journey.

What You Will Need

1-cm grid paper
tape
scissors

The Facts

• The oxen can pull a wagon filled with a maximum of 1800 lb of belongings and humans.

• Only two people at the most can ride in the front of the wagon at a time. A third person will have to walk. However, if someone is tired or sick, she or he can sleep in the back of the wagon. The average weight of a person in your party is 140 lb.

• Your wagon bed is 12 ft long, $3\frac{1}{2}$ ft wide and $2\frac{1}{2}$ ft high.

• Your back wheels are 5 ft in diameter. Your front wheels are about $3\frac{1}{2}$ ft in diameter. Circumference (***C***) equals $2\pi r$.

• Outside the wagon, a barrel or tar bucket can be attached to the back and one side. The toolbox can be attached to the other side.

• You can pack food into barrels. These barrels also can be filled with water for travel through the desert. Clothes can be packed into chests or bags.

• For extra meat, you can kill game on the trail and slaughter your cattle.

• You won't be able to buy goods when you get to the Oregon Territory, which is 2,000 miles away. But you can trade with other pioneers.

• Page 65 shows the items you can bring with you in the covered wagon. The larger items show dimensions along with weight.

Item	dimensions*	weight	Item	dimensions*	weight
1 comforter	72" x 44" x 2"	7 lb	**flour**	[All the food can be packed in 3–4 barrels.]	150 lb/person
1 feather bed	6' x 3' x 2"	15 lb	**pork and bacon**		25 lb/person
2 bread pans		1 lb	**coffee**		15 lb/person
kettle	1' d x 8" h	6 lb	**sugar**		20 lb/person
coffee pot		3 lb	**beans**		20 lb
fry pan		4 lb	**grain for cereal**		20 lb
5 sets silverware		1 lb	**dried fruit**		30 lb
5 tin cups		1 lb	**canned fruit**		10 lb
water bucket	1' d x 1' h	1 lb	**medicine**		1 lb
wash tub	2' x 1' x 1'	8 lb	**butter churn**	1' d x 3' h	4 lb
shovel	5' l x 9" w	2 lb	**clothing for 1 person**	[Each person's clothes can be packed in a chest or bags.]	10 lb/person
tar bucket for greasing axle	1' d x 2' h	15 lb	**bolt of cloth for sewing clothes**	30" x 14" x 4"	12 lb
tent		10 lb	**rocking chair- heirloom**	30" x 18" x .3'	29 lb
ground cloth		2 lb	**table—heirloom**	3' x 3' x 3'	35 lb
spade	42" l x 7" w		**quilt—heirloom**	6' x 4' x 6"	4 lb
soap		3 lb	**piano—heirloom**	5' x 2' x 3'	500 lb
ax	3' l x 6" w	1 lb	**headboard for a bed—heirloom**	4' h x 4' w x 3" deep	45 lb
hatchet	15" l x 6" w	2 lb	**grandfather clock—heirloom**	5' h x 15" w x 9" deep	100 lb
rifle	2' l	7 lb	**violin**	18" x 6" x 2"	$\frac{1}{2}$ lb
cradle	3' x 2' x 1'	25 lb	**Bible**		1 lb
toolbox	1' x 1' x 8"	12 lb	**4 books**	5" x 9" x 6"	4 lb
plow	6' x 2' x 3'	100 lb	**1 extra front wheel**	$3\frac{1}{2}$' d x $2\frac{1}{2}$" h	25 lb
barrel for storing food	2' d x 3' h	75 lb	**1 extra back wheel**	5' d x $2\frac{1}{2}$" h	30 lb
chest for clothes	3' x 2' x 2'	50 lb	**1 extra axle**	64" x 4" x 5"	20 lb
			extra wagon tongue	10' x 2" x 4"	10 lb

* Unless specified otherwise, dimensions are shown as length x width
x height. In addition, d = diameter, l = length, and h = height.

To Do List

- Use grid paper to make a scale model of the covered wagon bed and wheels. For your model, 1 cm equals 1 ft.
- Make a list of items you want to bring.
- Use grid paper to create the larger items you are thinking of bringing. Make them to scale. Include beds, chests, barrels, furniture, tubs, wheels, and so on.
- Show how you would pack the wagon.
- Record how much weight you have in the wagon altogether.
- Write an explanation of why you are taking some items and leaving others behind.

Extra

Figure out how many times the back wheel would turn on the journey.

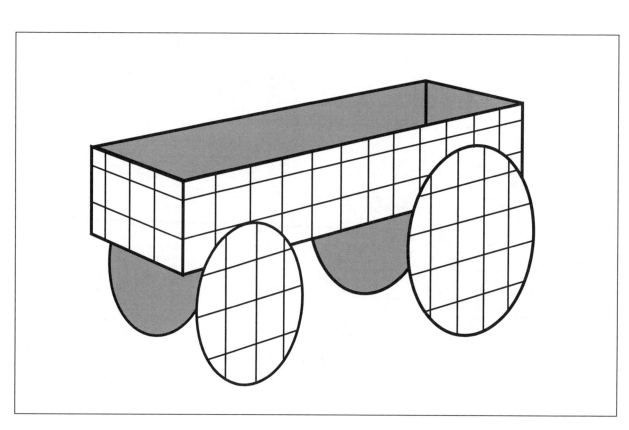

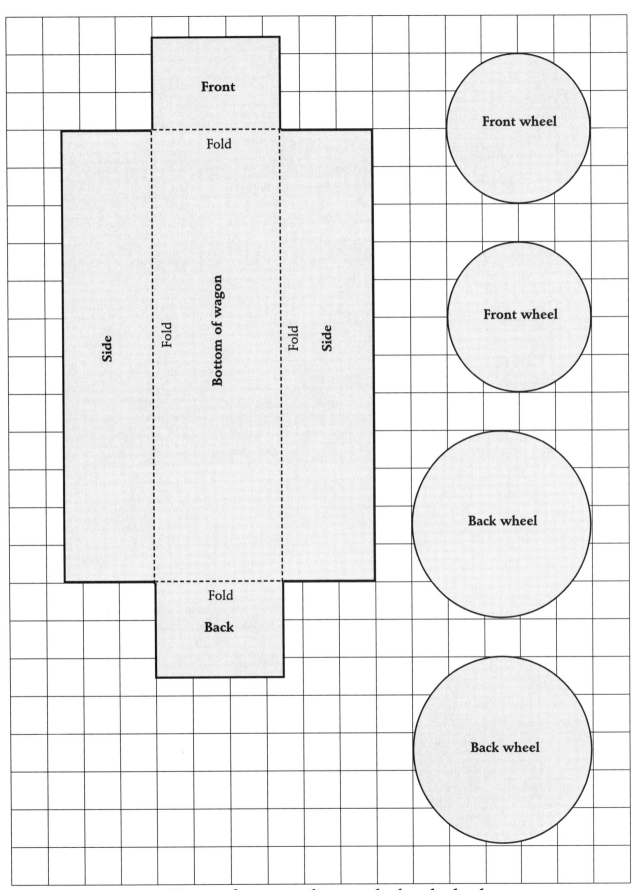

Pattern for covered wagon bed and wheels

CHAPTER 9

Home on
the Range

THE AMERICAN BUFFALO

Home on the Range
THE AMERICAN BUFFALO

The Challenge

Students create a visual display, such as a graph or picture, that shows the dramatic changes in the number of American buffalo from 1800 to the present. They make their visuals mathematically correct by showing the numbers of buffalo in proportion. The visuals also need to communicate the emotion and drama of the situation.

Extra: The American buffalo once roamed over about 1,250,000 square miles of grassland. Students need to find out the number of buffalo per square mile (or for the bad years, the number of square miles per buffalo) in 1800, 1850, 1889, 1950, and 1997. Students can use the number of buffalo per square mile as part of their visual displays.

Math Skills/Concepts

large numbers
visual representation of data
proportion

Materials

materials for visual displays

Background: Updated Buffalo Information

In 1872 Yellowstone National Park was set aside as a safe haven for a few hundred buffalo. But remarkably enough, people were allowed to shoot the animals in the park at that time, and hunters ended up destroying much of the herd by 1890. In 1894, a law was finally enacted making it illegal to kill buffalo in Yellowstone.

A little more than 100 years later, in 1997, between 3,000 and 4,000 buffalo made up the herd at Yellowstone National Park. When the grass became solidly frozen in the severe winter of 1997, some of the herd began leaving the park boundaries in search of food. Nearly 800 were killed by livestock officials trying to protect cattle ranches from a disease they believed could be transmitted from buffalo to cattle. Many people feared that the outrageous treatment of buffalo had started again.

On August 20, 1994, a white buffalo calf named Miracle was born in Wisconsin. Many Native Americans went to see her because ancient legend said that the spirit that created the bison would return as a white female buffalo, bringing peace and harmony with her.

Possible Solutions to the Challenge

Here are a few possibilities for visual displays:

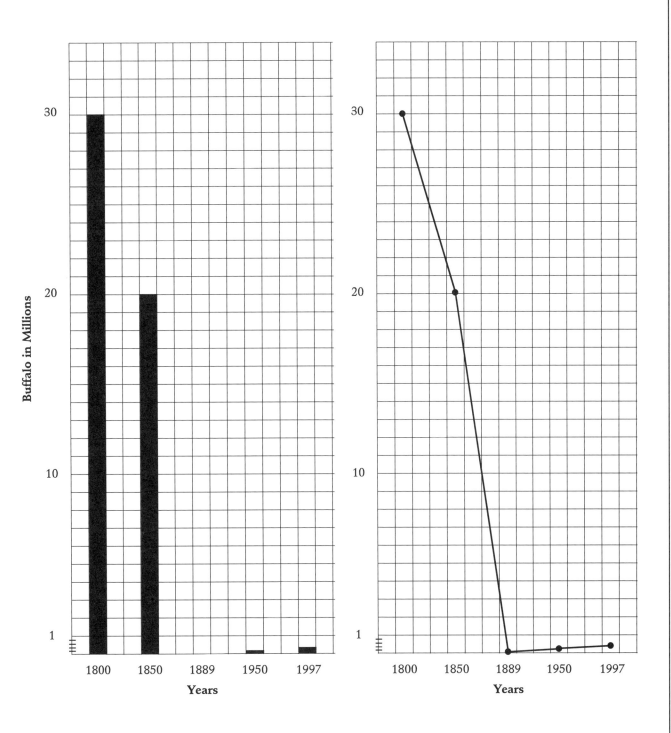

Buffalo in Millions

Years

30
20
10
1

1800   1850   1889   1950   1997

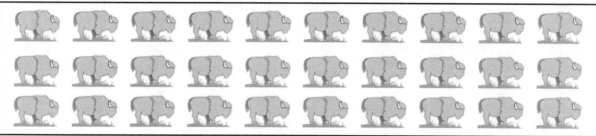 stands for 1 million buffalo

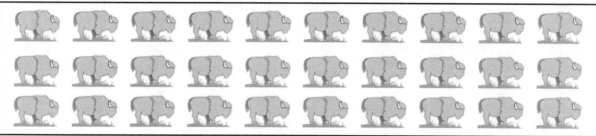

1800

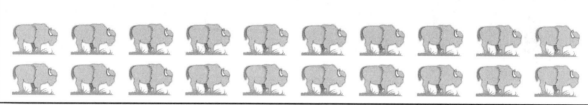

1850

1889

1950

1997

Extra: To find the number of buffalo per square mile (or square miles per buffalo), students need the fact that there used to be about 1,250,000 square miles of grassland. See the chart below:

Year	Number of Buffalo	Division	Answer
1800	40 million	40,000,000 ÷ 1,250,000 =	32 buffalo per sq mi
1850	20 million	20,000,000 ÷ 1,250,000 =	16 buffalo per sq mi
1889	Less than 1,000	1,250,000 ÷ 1,000 =	1,250 sq mi per buffalo
1950	25,000	1,250,000 ÷ 25,000 =	50 sq mi per buffalo
1997	200,000	1,250,000 ÷ 200,000 =	6.25 sq mi per buffalo

Questions

• In your display, how will you show the numbers of buffalo in proportion?
• Which piece of data is hardest to represent in proportion? (possibly 1,000 buffalo)

Extra:
• What numbers do you divide to find how many buffalo per square mile of grassland? (Divide the number of buffalo by the number of square miles.)
• What numbers do you divide to find how many square miles per buffalo? (Divide the number of square miles by the number of buffalo.)
• When the number of square miles per buffalo goes up, does it mean the number of buffalo has gone up or down? (down) Explain.

Home on the Range

THE AMERICAN BUFFALO

Introduction

"Buffalo were dark rich clouds moving upon the rolling hills and plains of America. And then the flashing steel came upon bone and flesh."
  Simon J. Ortiz, Acoma Pueblo poet*

50 Million Buffalo At least 30 million American buffalo, or bison, once roamed the plains of America and Canada. The Native Americans on the plains used them for nearly everything. They made leather clothing and tipis from the hides; buffalo robes and blankets from the fur; spoons, cups, and knives from the bones; bowstrings from the tendons; and musical instruments from the hooves. For

* Bryan Hodgson, "Buffalo: Home on the Range." *National Geographic*, November 1994, p. 68

Native Americans, the buffalo had special power, and a person who ate buffalo meat would gain that power. They worshipped the buffalo and thanked it for its gifts.

Less Than 1,000 Buffalo When the European fur traders started trading with the Native Americans for buffalo robes, the herds began decreasing. But when the railroad cut through buffalo country and anybody with a gun could shoot the buffalo, the slaughter truly

began. Some men shot at the buffalo for no better reason than to see them fall. Amateurs shot from railroad train windows. It became the thing to do. Professional hide hunters hurried West. Wild Bill Cody alone shot more than 4,280 buffalo in a year and a half. The government admittedly was trying to get rid of the Native Americans at that time and destroying the buffalo was one way to do it. By 1889, less than 1,000 buffalo remained!

"The destruction of Native people and the destruction of the environment are essentially the same."
Dagmar Thorpe, citizen of the Sauk and Fox Nation, director of Thakiwa Foundation*

200,000 Buffalo
Today, about 200,000 buffalo live on ranches and wildlife preserves in North America. Buffalo meat, with its low cholesterol, may be making a comeback. Some people are even proposing Buffalo Commons—nature preserves where buffalo can roam freely once again.

* Lois Crozier-Hogle and Darryl Babe Wilson, *Surviving in Two Worlds.* Austin, TX: University of Texas Press, 1997, p. 5.

The Challenge

Create a visual display, such as a graph or picture, that shows the dramatic changes in the number of American buffalo from 1800 to the present. Make your visual mathematically correct by showing the numbers of buffalo in proportion. The visual should also communicate some of the emotion and drama of the situation.

Extra: The American buffalo once roamed about 1,250,000 square miles of grassland. Calculate the number of buffalo per square mile (or for the bad years, the number of square miles per buffalo) in 1800, 1850, 1889, 1950, and 1997. You can use the number of buffalo per square mile as part of your visual display.

What You Will Need

materials for your visual display

The Facts

- In 1800 there were about 30,000,000 buffalo in North America.
- In 1850 there were about 20,000,000.
- In 1889 there were fewer than 1,000.
- In 1950 there were about 25,000.
- In 1997 there were about 200,000.
- Buffalo roamed in America and Alberta, Canada. They were found mainly in the area from the Rockies to the Appalachian Mountains and from Canada to Texas.

To Do List

- Decide on a way to create a visual display showing the dramatic changes in the numbers of buffalo for the years mentioned.
- Make sure you are displaying the numbers of buffalo in proportion. In other words, design your display so that, for example, 14 million buffalo looks twice as large as 7 million buffalo.
- Make sure your display conveys some of the emotion of the situation.

Extra:

Estimates show that the buffalo once roamed about 1,250,000 square miles of grassland.
- Calculate the number of buffalo per square mile of grassland in 1800 and 1850.
- Calculate the number of square miles of grassland per buffalo in 1889, 1950, and 1997.

CHAPTER 10
Eureka!

THE CALIFORNIA GOLD RUSH

Eureka!

THE CALIFORNIA GOLD RUSH

The Challenge

The gold seekers of the mid-1800s took their chances. The probability, or likelihood, of striking it rich were slim. In groups or pairs, students create a game of chance using a California gold rush theme. They figure out the probability of winning their game. Then they test their game and record the outcomes. The class holds a Gold Rush Festival using all the games in the classroom. Students keep track of outcomes from their games.

Extra: Students compare the mathematical probability of winning their games to the experimental probability of winning them.

Note: If your students haven't studied probability, have them design board games using the numerical facts about the gold rush and one or more mathematical operations.

Math Skills/Concepts
probability

Materials
materials for making games of chance

Background: Diversity in the Gold Rush
Not all people who rushed to California were white males. Women came by themselves and with their husbands. These women mined, set up businesses, entertained, taught, gambled, cooked, became bankers, and more. One woman made $900 in nine weeks by doing laundry for the miners. Some women, like Mammy (Mary Ellen) Pleasant, did

very well for themselves. Mammy, who was an African American, set up a restaurant, invested money in real estate, and helped in the antislavery movement. Another woman, Dame Shirley, became famous for her letters describing mining life.

Many Chinese, who called California the "Golden Mountain," came in search of gold. Of all the miners, they were the most unjustly treated, even being forced out of the best mining areas. But these Chinese miners were courageous. By 1860 they numbered 285,000, and they went on to have a significant influence in the city of San Francisco and throughout the state.

Possible Solutions to the Challenge
Here are descriptions of sample games of chance:

Penny Toss or Stick Toss

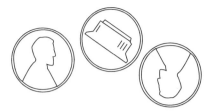

Materials: 2 or 3 pennies (or 2 or 3 tongue depressors with a design on one side)
- Player flips 2 or 3 pennies that represent gold-panning pans. Heads (H) means gold. Tails (T) means an empty pan.
- The possible outcomes are

Two pennies	HH, TT, TH, HT
Three pennies	HHH, TTT, THH, TTH, THT, HTH, HTT, HHT

- Player wins if he or she gets 2 H in the two-penny toss, or 3 H in the three-penny toss.
- For the two-penny toss, the chance of getting 2H or 2T is $\frac{1}{4}$ and of getting 1T1H is $\frac{1}{2}$.
- For the three-penny toss, the chances of getting 3H or 3T is $\frac{1}{8}$, of getting 2H1T is $\frac{3}{8}$, and of getting 2T1H is $\frac{3}{8}$.

Dice Roll

Materials: 2 dice
- Player tosses dice and finds sum. Player finds gold if he or she rolls a 2 or a 12.
- Possible outcomes are

2 1+1
3 1+2, 2+1
4 1+3, 2+2, 3+1
5 1+4, 2+3, 3+2, 4+1
6 1+5, 2+4, 3+3, 4+2, 5+1
7 1+6, 2+5, 3+4, 4+3, 5+2, 6+1
8 2+6, 3+5, 4+4, 5+3, 6+2
9 3+6, 4+5, 5+4, 6+3
10 4+6, 5+5, 6+4
11 5+6, 6+5
12 6+6

or

+	1	2	3	4	5	6
1	2	3	4	5	6	7
2	3	4	5	6	7	8
3	4	5	6	7	8	9
4	5	6	7	8	9	10
5	6	7	8	9	10	11
6	7	8	9	10	11	12

- The probability of rolling 2 or 12 is $\frac{1}{36}$; of rolling 3 or 11 is $\frac{2}{36}$ or $\frac{1}{18}$; of rolling 4 or 10 is $\frac{3}{36}$ or $\frac{1}{12}$; of rolling 5 or 9 is $\frac{4}{36}$ or $\frac{1}{9}$; of rolling 6 or 8 is $\frac{5}{36}$; and of rolling 7 is $\frac{6}{36}$ or $\frac{1}{6}$.

Spinneroo

Materials: 1 homemade spinner of varying design
- Player spins the spinner to find out how many gold nuggets were found.
- The possible outcomes are
  1, 1, 2, 2, 3, 4, 5, 8.
- Player wins if he or she spins 8.
- The probability of spinning 3 or 8 is $\frac{1}{8}$, and of spinning 1, 2, or 4 is $\frac{1}{4}$.

- The possible outcomes are 1, 2, and 3.
- Player wins if he or she spins 3.
- The probability of spinning 3 is $\frac{1}{8}$, of spinning 1 is $\frac{1}{2}$, and of spinning are 2 is $\frac{3}{8}$.

Gold in a Bag

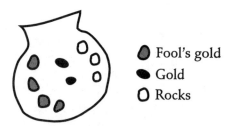

- Fool's gold
- Gold
- Rocks

Materials: chips or marbles in 3 or more colors
- Player pulls a piece from the bag.
- The possible outcomes are

- Player wins if he or she pulls out a nugget of gold.
- The probability of pulling out gold is $\frac{2}{9}$ of pulling out fool's gold is $\frac{4}{9}$, and of pulling out a rock is $\frac{3}{9}$, or $\frac{1}{3}$.

Tack or Paper Clip Toss

Materials: 3–5 tacks or bent paper clips
- Player tosses the tacks or paper clips.
- The possible outcomes are: **DDD, UUU, DDU, DUD, UDD, UUD, UDU, DUU** where D = Down and U = Up.
- Player finds gold, buys a new pair of boots and wins if he or she gets 3 paper clips Up or 3 Down.
- After tossing 3 tacks, the experimental probability of 3 Up or Down is about $\frac{15}{100}$ or $\frac{3}{20}$; of 2 out of 3 Up is about $\frac{30}{100}$, or $\frac{3}{10}$; and of 1 out of 3 Up is about $\frac{55}{100}$, or $\frac{11}{20}$.
- After tossing 3 paper clips, the experimental probability of 3 Up or Down is about $\frac{20}{100}$, or $\frac{1}{5}$; of 2 out of 3 Up is about $\frac{20}{100}$, or $\frac{1}{5}$; and of 1 out of 3 is about $\frac{60}{100}$, or $\frac{1}{5}$.

Weighted Cube Roll

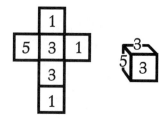

Materials: handmade die with less than six numbers on its sides

- Two players take turns rolling the die.
- The possible outcomes are 1, 1, 1, 3, 3, 5.
- Player gets 5 gold nugget points if he or she rolls a 5. Player gets 3 gold nugget points for a 3, and 1 point for a 1. First player to get 25 gold nugget points wins.
- Probability of rolling 5 is $\frac{1}{6}$, of rolling 1 is $\frac{1}{2}$, and of rolling 3 is $\frac{1}{3}$.

Irregular Shape Toss

Materials: handmade prism or square pyramid
- Player tosses the shape.
- The possible outcomes are **T, T, T, S** for the pyramid and **S, S, S, S, S, S, H, H** for the hexagonal prism, where T=triangle, S=square, H=hexagon.
- Player finds a glassful of gold (worth $1,000) and wins if he or she tosses a T or an S.
- For the pyramid, the experimental probability of getting a triangle is about $\frac{60}{100}$, or $\frac{3}{5}$, and of getting the square base is about $\frac{40}{100}$, or $\frac{2}{5}$. For the prism, the experimental probability of getting a square is about $\frac{40}{100}$, or $\frac{2}{5}$, and of getting a hexagonal base is about $\frac{60}{100}$, or $\frac{3}{5}$.

2 Spinneroo

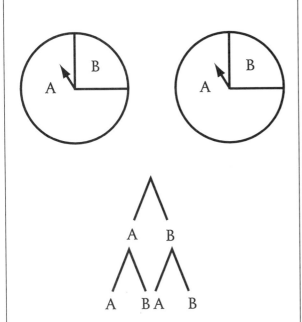

A   B

A   BA   B

Example: Probability of AA is   x   =

Materials: 2 handmade spinners
- 1. Player spins both spinners.
- The possible outcomes are
  AA, BB, AB, BA.
- Player strikes it rich and wins if he or she spins BB.

The chances of BB are $\frac{1}{16}$.

The chances of AB are $\frac{3}{16}$.

The chances of BA are $\frac{3}{16}$.

The chances of AA are $\frac{9}{16}$.

Questions
- How can you be sure you have all possible outcomes? (Record possible outcomes in an organized way.)
- Why is this an incomplete list of possible outcomes for two pennies: HH, TT, TH? (HT was left out.)
- How will you find the probability of each outcome? (Find the ratio of a specific outcome to all the possible outcomes.)
- What will the sum of the probabilities of all outcomes be? (1)
- How will you decide what makes a winning roll or toss? (the most unlikely outcome[s])
- Why would it be difficult to find the mathematical probability for tossing a tack or a pyramid shape? (They are not a regular shape like a cube. They don't have equally likely outcomes, such as heads and tails.)

Eureka!

THE CALIFORNIA GOLD RUSH

> "We went again to the canion to find that bewitching ore that is called gold. We had better luck in finding it to day, my husband & I making 16 dollars in fine dust."
>
> Lucena Parsons*
>
> *Joanne Levy, *They Saw the Elephant*. Hamden, CT: (Archon Books) The Shoe String Press, 1990, p. 110.

> "Of course, if one thought to find gold here easily, that was a mistake, for although there are opportunities here to gain great wealth, it depends on luck and chance. . . . We dug and washed dirt for a whole week and found only $8.00 worth of gold. . . ."
>
> Joseph Francl, Placerville, February 3, 1855
>
> * Joseph Francl, *The Overland Journey of Joseph Francl*. San Francisco, CA: William P. Wreden, 1968, pp. 50, 52.

> "We have worked eight days and have made $16,000—we have had extremely good luck."
>
> Robert and Charles Springer*
>
> * Walker D. Wyman, ed., *California Emigrant Letters*. New York, NY: Bookman Associates, 1952, p. 78.

Introduction

Native Americans undoubtedly knew that gold existed in California well before the gold rush. Many reports also show that Mexicans found gold deposits throughout California as early as 1828. But it was on January 24, 1848, when carpenter James Marshall discovered a piece of gold worth about 50 cents at John Sutter's sawmill, that "gold fever" took hold. The news traveled quickly by newspaper and word of mouth after President James Polk announced that gold had been found in California. Fortune seekers, called *forty-niners* (it was 1849 by then), came from all over the world—the eastern United States, Chile, Mexico, China, Ireland, England, Hawaii, Australia, and elsewhere. Those who came were mostly men, but one of every 100 was a woman.

In one year, the non-Native American population of California grew from about 14,000 to about 100,000. The city of San Francisco swelled from about 900 people to about 25,000. Some of the forty-niners struck it rich, some went home with nothing to show for their trouble, and some died in pursuit of their dreams. Luck and chance played a big part.

The Challenge

The gold seekers took their chances. The probability, or chance, of striking it rich was slim. In groups or pairs, create a game of chance using a California gold rush theme. Figure out the probability of winning your game. Test your game and record the results. As a class, hold a Gold Rush Festival using all the games and keep track of all the results from your game.

Extra: Compare the mathematical probability of win-

ning your game to the experimental probability of winning it.

Note: If you haven't studied probability yet, design a board game using the numerical facts about the gold rush and one or more mathematical operations.

What You Will Need

materials for creating gold rush games of chance

The Facts About the Gold Rush

• The journey to California was dangerous. It could be made across the desert by covered wagon, by sea around the tip of South America, or by land and sea through the jungles of Panama. Disease, accidents, starvation, and natural disasters took many lives.
• Living conditions in California were crude. Miners slept in tents, shacks, and caves or out in the open. They cooked outside.

The California Gold Rush **83**

- Problems in mining camps sometimes led to fighting, stealing, and murder.
- A pinch of gold was worth about $1, an ounce about $17, a small glass about $100, and a large glass about $1,000.
- Miners were lucky to mine 1 ounce a day.
- Supplies were very expensive. A dozen eggs could cost $10; potatoes were $1 each; half a pound of cheese was $6; bread $2; and boots $100.
- Among the most successful people were merchants who sold goods to miners. One was Levi Strauss who sold denim pants!
- Methods for mining gold included panning, using a cradle, using a Long Tom or sluice boxes, building dams, hydraulic mining, and hard rock mining.

The Facts About Probability and Games of Chance

Here is an example of a game of chance.

Two-Chip Toss

Materials: 2 chips with one side red (R) and one side white (W)
- Player tosses the chips, which are gold (not fool's gold). The player wins if RR is tossed.
- Possible outcomes are RR, WW, RW, WR.
- Probability of 2R or 2W is $\frac{1}{4}$ each. Probability of 1R1W is $\frac{1}{2}$.

Extra: If you have one coin to toss, you can find the mathematical probability of getting heads, which is 1 out of 2, or $\frac{1}{2}$, without touching the coin.
You can also find the experimental probability of getting heads by flipping the coin approximately 100 times or more and recording the results.

To Do List

- Design a game of chance with a gold rush theme. Here are some materials you could use:

  2 or 3 pennies

  1, 2, or 3 standard dice

  1 or 2 spinners

  1, 2, or 3 tongue depressors with a design on one side

  chips or marbles of different colors to be drawn from a bag

  1 or 2 weighted dice (with the same number on more than one side)

  homemade cards or a deck of cards

  3, 4, or 5 tacks or bent paper clips

  irregular shape (such as a square pyramid or a prism)

- Write directions for your game.
- Record all the possible outcomes of your game.
- Find the mathematical probability of winning your game and the experimental probability of getting all other outcomes. (If you can't do this because you are using an irregular shape, such as a tack or a pyramid, make predictions about the probability of each outcome.)
- Try your game at least 25 to 100 times. Record your outcomes.
- Have a Gold Rush Festival. Try each other's games of chance. Keep track of all outcomes when your classmates play your game.

Extra: Gather all the results you have—the outcomes from your own testing and from the festival. Compare the mathematical probability of winning your game to the experimental probability of winning your game. Write about it. (In the case of irregular shapes, compare your prediction to the experimental probability and write about it.)

CHAPTER 11
A "Train" to Freedom

THE UNDERGROUND RAILROAD

A "Train" to Freedom
THE UNDERGROUND RAILROAD

The Challenge

Using maps of the Underground Railroad, students work in pairs or groups to find the number of routes to freedom. The students' main task will be to identify the total number of routes on Map 2 which shows only the eastern and southeastern United States. For more of a challenge, they can find the total number of routes to freedom on Map 1, which includes all the states and territories of the United States in 1860 (see page 90). Using overheads of the maps, students share results and make sure they have found every route. Note that a route runs from a small circle to an arrow.

Extra: Students find the total number of routes going north on Map 3 (see page 93), which shows some of the Underground Railroad routes through Ohio.

Math Skills/Concepts
discrete math
routing

Materials
colored pens or pencils (optional)
overheads of the maps for checking results

Background: How the Underground Railroad Worked

The slaves who escaped from the slave states often depended on the North Star and rivers (which mainly flowed north) to guide them to freedom. Armed with their own ingenuity and determination, they made their way to the free states in the North. By the early 1830s, what was known as the Underground Railroad was in place to assist them.

Along the way, stations and conductors on this trackless train offered safe places to stay. Stations were people's homes, churches, and other spots such as caves where free African Americans, Quakers, and other station masters put out signals such as a lantern, candle, quilt, or flag to let fugitive slaves know that they had found a safe resting place.

Slaves walked between 10 and 30 miles a night. Conductors smuggled them on boats and wagons. From 30,000 to 100,000 slaves traveled on the Underground Railroad. The number is hard to pin-point because records, which would have been incriminating, are scarce.

The most famous conductor was Harriet Tubman who, after escaping, helped approximately 300 slaves to freedom. By 1860, $40,000 was offered for her capture. For a beautiful telling of her story and many other aspects of the Underground Railroad, encourage students to read *Get on Board, The Story of the Underground Railroad* by Jim Haskins (Scholastic, 1993).

Possible Solutions to the Challenge

• Map 2 (page 92) shows 9 possible routes going south from Georgia and Florida. There are 12 possible routes going north. Students can find and count each route one by one, or they can multiply the number of starting points by the number of ending arrows.

Example:

3 x 3 = 9 routes

• Students have already found the 21 routes on the right side of Map 1. In addition, 4 routes leave Texas, and 1 leaves Missouri. In the middle of the map, a large grouping of routes goes north. In this group, one starting point in Alabama is a little confusing; unlike the others, only 1 possible route goes north from here. The rest of the routes in this grouping can be found one at a time. Or students can multiply the 7 starting points by the 5 ending arrows to get 35 routes. Thus there are

21 + 4 + 1 + 1 + 35 = 62 routes

in all on Map 1.

• Map 3 (page 93) shows 11 routes going north. Students can describe each route by using a series of letters. Students will have to find an organized way to approach the problem, such as taking one starting point and finding all the routes going north from that point. Using differently colored pens or pencils to trace the routes might also be helpful. All the routes on Map 3 are shown at the bottom of the page.

Questions

• How can you group the arrows on Maps 1 and 2? (You can group the arrows that are connected together.)
• On Maps 1 and 2, what strategy did you use to find the routes? Were you able to find a shortcut? (In some groups of routes on the map, you can multiply the number of starting points times the number of ending arrows to find the total number of routes.)

Extra:

• What is tricky about Map 3? (There are many ways to go north from B or from C to get to F.)
• On Map 3, what will your strategy be? Where will you start? (Students may want to find all the possible routes beginning with AB and all the possible routes beginning with AC. They can also divide the routes into those ending with the arrow G and those ending with the arrow H.)

	Ending at Arrow G	Ending at Arrow H
Starting with A B	ABDFG	
	ABDEFG	ABDEH
	ABCEFG	
	ABCDFG	ABCDEH
Starting with A C	ACDFG	
	ACDEFG	ACDEH
	ACEFG	ACEH

A "Train" to Freedom

THE UNDERGROUND RAILROAD

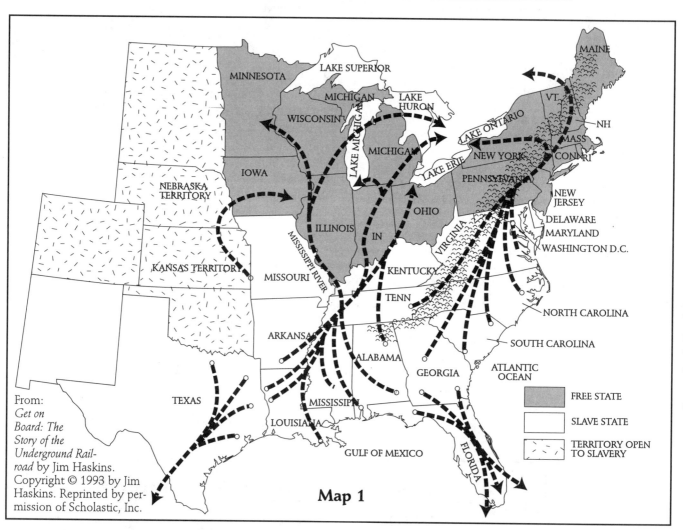

From:
Get on Board: The Story of the Underground Railroad by Jim Haskins. Copyright © 1993 by Jim Haskins. Reprinted by permission of Scholastic, Inc.

FREE STATE

SLAVE STATE

TERRITORY OPEN TO SLAVERY

Map 1

Introduction

Map 1 shows routes to freedom on the Underground Railroad. As you can see from this map, fugitive slaves traveled north, but they also escaped to the Caribbean, Mexico, and Africa.

In 1996 Anthony Cohen, a 32-year-old African American historian, set off from Maryland for a two-month journey along one of the routes of the Underground Railroad. His destination was Ontario, Canada, where many escaped slaves found the freedom for which they had

risked their lives. (They went to Canada because laws were passed in the United States making it a crime to help them and allowing slave owners to bring slaves back from the free Northern states.)

Cohen stopped at places along the way that had been stations on the

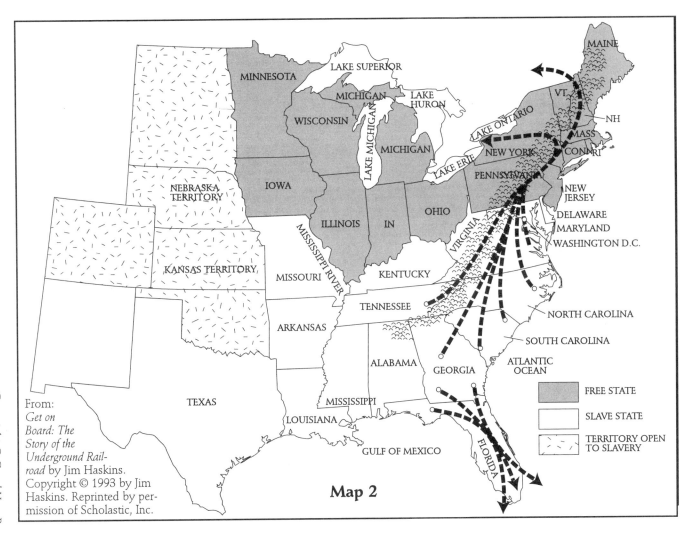

MAINE

VT.

NH

LAKE SUPERIOR

MINNESOTA

MICHIGAN

LAKE HURON

WISCONSIN

LAKE MICHIGAN

MICHIGAN

LAKE ONTARIO

MASS

NEW YORK

CONN RI

LAKE ERIE

PENNSYLVANIA

NEW JERSEY

NEBRASKA TERRITORY

IOWA

DELAWARE

MARYLAND

WASHINGTON D.C.

ILLINOIS

IN

OHIO

VIRGINIA

MISSISSIPPI RIVER

KANSAS TERRITORY

MISSOURI

KENTUCKY

NORTH CAROLINA

TENNESSEE

SOUTH CAROLINA

ARKANSAS

ALABAMA

ATLANTIC OCEAN

GEORGIA

TEXAS

MISSISSIPPI

LOUISIANA

FLORIDA

GULF OF MEXICO

Map 2

From:
Get on Board: The Story of the Underground Railroad by Jim Haskins. Copyright © 1993 by Jim Haskins. Reprinted by permission of Scholastic, Inc.

FREE STATE

SLAVE STATE

TERRITORY OPEN TO SLAVERY

Underground Railroad. Many of these places had been homes and churches of free African Americans who put their freedom at risk, and of Quakers (and people from other religious groups) who risked being jailed. Hiding places for the courageous slaves included homes and barns with trap doors, false walls, secret passages, attics, and cellars. They also hid in secret tunnels and caves.

Cohen made his way on foot (averaging 10 to 25 miles a day), by boat, and by train. At one point he shipped himself in a box by rail to reenact the experience of Henry (Box) Brown, the slave who spent 26 hours in a box that he had shipped to the Anti-Slavery Society in Philadelphia. A woman, Lear Green, transported herself in the same way.

In his journal Cohen describes reaching Canada and freedom: "I grasped the Canadian soil and for a good five to eight minutes, I cried."

The Challenge

Using maps of the Underground Railroad, work in pairs or groups to find the number of routes to freedom. Your main task is to find the total number of routes on Map 2 of the Underground Railroad shown here. This map includes only routes in the eastern and southeastern United States. A more challenging task is to calculate the total number of routes to freedom on Map 1, which shows routes

throughout the states and territories of the United States in 1860 (see page 90). Share your results with the class, and work together to make sure every route has been found.

Extra: Find the total number of routes going north on Map 3 on page 93, which traces some of the Underground Railroad routes through Ohio.

The Facts

Map 2 shows routes to freedom on the Underground Railroad in the eastern and southeastern United States.

Examples of routes:

A route begins at a dot and ends at an arrow.

There are two routes here, AB and AC.

There are two routes here, AC and BC.

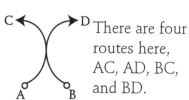
There are four routes here, AC, AD, BC, and BD.

Extra Facts: Map 3 shows some of the many Underground Railroad routes in Ohio. The Ohio River was a boundary between slave and free states. How many routes to freedom are shown? When finding them, you can only move northward (north, northeast, northwest).

What You Will Need

colored pens or pencils (optional)

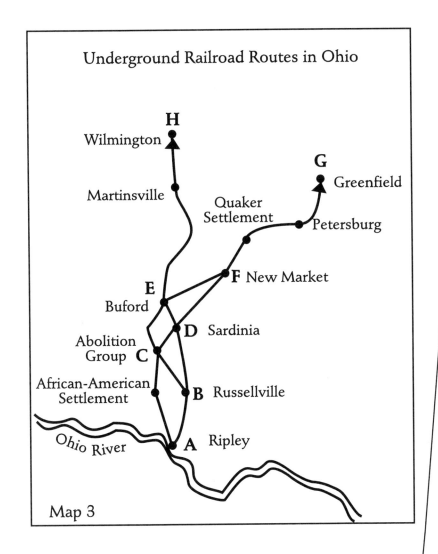

Underground Railroad Routes in Ohio

H
Wilmington

Martinsville

Quaker
Settlement

G
Greenfield

Petersburg

F New Market

E
Buford

D Sardinia

Abolition
Group   C

African-American
Settlement

B Russellville

Ohio River

A   Ripley

Map 3

To Do List

- On Map 2, identify all the different routes to freedom. Write about your strategy for finding them. Did you discover a shorter method for counting routes? Explain.

- On Map 1, find and record all the different routes to freedom. Write about your strategy for finding them. Did you discover a shorter method? Explain.

Extra: On Map 3, find and record all the different routes to freedom. Did you find them in an organized way? Explain.

CHAPTER 12
The Mail Must Go Through

THE PONY EXPRESS

The Mail Must Go Through

THE PONY EXPRESS

The Challenge

The students in your class have been selected to plan a reenactment of the Pony Express, using the members of the class as riders. Using a map and facts about speed and endurance, students figure out how many horses and riders are necessary. Then they assign riders to each part of the route.

Extra: Students create a detailed, day-by-day schedule of riders and horses.

Math Skills/Concepts

ratio
rate
scale

Materials

ruler

Background: The Nitty-Gritty of the Pony Express

The Pony Express covered 1,966 miles, with stations every 10 to 15 miles along the way and a home station every 75 to 100 miles. Riders rode back and forth between their home stations. The average age of riders was 22, and they were paid well for those days. In the short history of the Pony Express, one pony rider was killed.

The actual schedule they had to keep is on page 97.

The terrain in Missouri and Nebraska is mostly flat plains. Wyoming has flat plains in the east, then the Rockies, and then dry, treeless plains in the

west. Utah and Nevada are mostly desert. Starting in Carson City, Nevada, the route traverses the Sierra Nevada range.

Possible Solutions to the Challenge

• Students can use the scale on the map (1 in. = 200 mi) to figure out the length of the route. They will need to triple the distance they measure between Carson City and Sacramento because of the twisty mountain passes. They will probably come up with about 1,650 miles (1,200 miles on plains and deserts and 450 miles in the mountains).
• From the length of the route, students can figure out how many riders are needed. Since riders go approximately 100 miles per day, students will need about 17 riders.
• Since horses go only about 15 miles and riders go about 100 miles, each rider will need 7 horses. The class will need about 119 horses in all.
• Some students will figure out how long the trip will take by dividing the 1,650 miles of the journey by 10 miles per hour, to get 165 hours, or about 7 days. Other students will try to be more precise

A Real Pony Express Schedule

St. Joseph to Kearney	34 hours
Kearney to Laramie	46 hours
Laramie to Salt Lake City	44 hours
Salt Lake City to Carson City	64 hours
Carson City to Sacramento	46 hours
Total	234 hours

by taking the flat and mountainous terrain into account. For example, approximately 1,200 miles at 10 miles per hour is about 120 hours. Approximately 450 miles at 7 miles per hour is about 64 hours. Calculating this way, students will find that it takes about 184 hours, or about 8 days to cover the Pony Express route.

Extra: To make the schedule, students can mark off each rider's segment of the route on the map. The segments can be labeled with numbers or letters. The numbers can be used on the schedule of rider assignments to show which rider is responsible for each part of the route.

Questions

• Why is it important to find the length of the route first? How does the scale of the map help you? Why do you triple the distance in the mountains?

• How will you figure out how many riders and horses are needed?

• How will you show the different riders' assignments on the map?

• Will the assignments you give riders be equal, or will you take into account the terrain?

• How does the speed of the horses help you figure out how long the trip will take? What does 10 miles per hour mean?

The Mail Must Go Through

THE PONY EXPRESS

Introduction

The Pony Express lasted a mere 18 months, from April 1860 to October 1861. During that time, the job of a pony rider was both dangerous and glamorous. The riders carried mail between St. Joseph, Missouri, and Sacramento, California. (At the time, telegraph wires from the East Coast ended in St. Joseph.) Riders had to keep to a strict schedule, regardless of storms, snow-capped mountains, scorching deserts, icy streams, horse thieves, and attacks by Native Americans whose land was being invaded.

The Challenge

Your class has been selected to plan a reenactment of the Pony Express using your classmates as riders. Using a map and facts about speed and endurance, figure out how many horses and riders you will need. Then assign riders to each part of the route. Good luck!

Extra: Make a detailed, day-by-day schedule of riders and horses.

What You Will Need

ruler

The Facts About the Ride

• The route runs between St. Joseph, Missouri, and Sacramento, California.
• After you measure the distance from Carson City to Sacramento, triple it to account for the twisty mountain passes.
• The trip can take no more than 8 to 10 days. Riders will ride day and night.
• One rider can ride about 100 miles. (To be more precise, a rider on the plains and desert can ride about 120 miles, and a rider in the mountains can ride about 55 miles.)
• Many times along the way, a rider will stop at stations to change horses.

• One horse can travel about 15 miles.
• The horses travel at an average speed of 10 miles per hour. However, they are lucky if they can travel 7 miles per hour in the steep Sierra Nevada.

The Facts About the Terrain

• The plains are the easiest part of the route.
• The desert in Utah and Nevada is the loneliest part of the route. There, the dust is acid and the heat is often devastating. The ground is sandy and rocky.
• The treacherous, steep mountain grades and snow-capped peaks of the Sierra Nevada mountains are the most difficult part of the route.

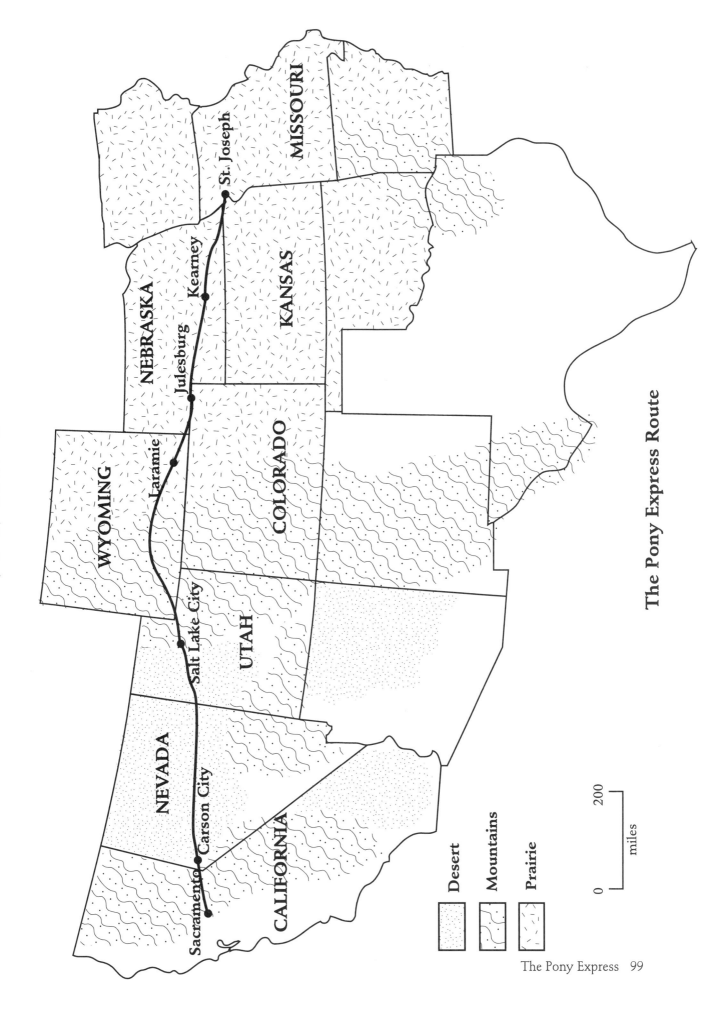

The Pony Express Route

Desert

Mountains

Prairie

0   200
miles

To Do List

- Find the length of the route. You will start in St. Joseph and travel west to Sacramento.
- Figure out how many riders and horses you will need.
- List the names of the riders (your classmates). Find jobs for other classmates. Everyone should have a job.
- Assign riders, by name, to the various parts of the route. Who will brave the prairie? the desert? the mountainous areas? Find a way to show where the assignments fall on the map.
- Figure out how long the trip will take.

Extra:

- Make a detailed, day-by-day schedule of riders and horses, taking into account the terrain they will be crossing. (Your starting date is a week from today.)
- Write an explanation of the strategies you used for creating the schedule.

CHAPTER 13
Lady Liberty

IMMIGRATION AND THE STATUE OF LIBERTY

Copyright © Good Year Books

Lady Liberty

IMMIGRATION AND THE STATUE OF LIBERTY

The Challenge

Students consider the question: "What if the Statue of Liberty were modeled after me?" For example, if they have long arms, the statue would have long arms too. They calculate dimensions of this personal Statue of Liberty using their own measurements and using only the height of the real statue. When they are finished, they compare the measurements they came up with to the measurements of the real Statue of Liberty created by the French sculptor Frédéric Auguste Bartholdi in 1886.

Extra: Students make scale drawings of their personal Statues of Liberty.

Math Skills/Concepts

ratio and proportion, scale
division
fractions and decimals

Materials

2 pieces of 1-cm grid paper taped together
   lengthwise
calculator
tape

Background: Immigrants Then and Now

America has been a place of freedom for many immigrants throughout history. From 1880 to 1920, 23 million immigrants came to America, mostly from Europe. Those coming by ship had to pass through Ellis Island, where they were examined and questioned. Most were allowed to enter the United States, some had to wait on the island because of sickness, and some were sent back.

Immigrants fled persecution, wars, and natural disaster in their homelands. They came for religious and political freedom, for better wages, to own land, and more. Some had heard that "the streets were paved in gold." Many changed their names, or had them changed by officials, when they entered the country.

In 1917 a law was passed requiring immigrants to be able to read in some language. In this way, some Americans tried to exclude immigrants they felt were uneducated. In the 1920s other laws were passed to restrict the number of immigrants admitted to the country.

Debates still rage about immigration. But America is, and always will be, a nation of immigrants. Some people have predicted that by the middle of the twenty-first century, less than half of all Americans will be of European descent. In 1997 there were already more than 2 million multiracial children in the United States, including the famous golfer Tiger Woods. The fact that we are all from different places makes America richer.

Possible Solutions to the Challenge

Here are two possible methods for meeting the challenge: finding the scale factor by division or using ratio and proportion. Note that when measuring themselves, students can round to the nearest foot and inch. Or they can convert fractions of a foot to decimals by dividing with a calculator and rounding (e.g., 5'4" = $5\frac{1}{3}$" = 5.33' = 5.3'). Some students may decide to use centimeters and meters instead.

1. Division (finding the scale factor)
Assume the student is 5'4", or 5.3', tall. Then the statue is
111' ÷ 5.3' = 20.9 times as tall as the student. After taking his or her measurements for arm length, eye width, and so on, the student can multiply every measurement by 20.9.

2. Ratio and Proportion
The student can use ratio and proportion for each measurement as shown in this example.

$$\frac{\text{Student height}}{\text{statute height}} = \frac{\text{student arm}}{X} \qquad \frac{5.3'}{111'} \qquad \frac{2'}{X}$$

$$X = 41.8'$$

The statue's arm is about 42 feet long.

Extra: To make a scale drawing of the head, arm, and hand of their personal Statues of Liberty, students can use centimeter grid paper, and a scale of 1 cm = 2 ft.

Questions

• How can you find other measurements on your personal Statue of Liberty knowing the real statue's height and your height? (by finding the scale factor or using ratio and proportion)

• What will you multiply each of your measurements by to get your statue's measurements? (See possible solutions.) Or, how can you set up a proportion using your height and the actual statue's height? (See possible solutions.)

• Why is a calculator helpful for this project? (for dividing to find the scale factor and for changing fractions to decimals)

Extra: How can you use the scale 1 cm = 2 ft (or 1 cm = 61 cm) to make your scale drawing?

The dimensions of the real Statue of Liberty are as follows:

	Standard Measurements	Metric Measurements
Height	111 ft	33.83 m
Height of head	17 ft	5.18 m
Head, from ear to ear	10 ft	3.05 m
Length of right arm	42 ft	12.80 m
Length of hand	16.5 ft	5.03 m
Length of index finger	8 ft	2.43 m
Length and width of fingernail	13 in. x 10 in.	33 cm x 25 cm
Width of eyes	2.5 ft	76 cm or .76 m
Width of mouth	3 ft	91 cm or .91 m
Length of nose	4.5 ft	1.37 m

1 cm = 2 feet

Lady Liberty

Immigration and the Statue of Liberty

Introduction

Listen to the voices of recent immigrants to the United States:*

"My parents say, 'You come from a different background, so to get ahead you have to do twice if not three times better than the American-born person."
Tito, age 14, Mexican

* Janet Bode, *New Kids in Town*. New York, NY: Scholastic, 1989, pp. 70 and 121.

"Today it is September and I am starting university. I am a very lucky person. And when my family gets here and we are together again, we will make such a celebration!"
Von, age 20, Vietnamese

As you can tell from the quotes here, being an immigrant in America today has its ups and downs. It wasn't easy for the immigrants who came to America from Europe between 1820 and the 1920s, either. Millions came across the Atlantic. Most of them came into New York Harbor, past the Statue of Liberty to Ellis Island.

"I will never forget the joy I felt when I saw . . . the Statue of Liberty after so many dark days on board the crowded ship," said one immigrant.†

The Statue of Liberty, which served as a symbol of freedom to so many immigrants, was designed by French sculptor Frédéric Auguste Bartholdi as a gift to America. Before building the statue, workers made sketches and models. One model was one-quarter size. Workers then erected an iron frame and created the statue in 10 different sections. Completed in Paris, France, the 151-foot statue was taken apart and shipped in 214 crates to New York. The pedestal being built in the United States could not be finished until $100,000 was finally raised to pay for it. A celebration to unveil the statue took place on October 28,

1886. A young boy was supposed to give the sculptor the signal to drop the French flag hiding the statue's eyes. The boy gave the signal before the speaker was finished, but the crowd never knew the difference. The statue has been the symbol of liberty ever since.

By the way, where did your family come from?

The Challenge

What if the Statue of Liberty had been modeled after you? Then, if you have long arms, the statue would have long arms too. Using only the height of the actual stat-

ue, calculate the dimensions of your personal Statue of Liberty based on your measurements. When you are finished, compare the measurements you came up with to the measurements of the real Statue of Liberty created by the French sculptor. **Extra:** Make a scale drawing of your personal Statue of Liberty.

What You Will Need

2 pieces of centimeter grid
   paper taped together
   lengthwise
calculator
tape

† William E. Shapiro, *The Statue of Liberty, A First Book*. New York, NY: Franklin Watts, 1985.

The Facts

- The Statue of Liberty is about 111 feet (33.83 meters) from head to toe.
- The longest ray on her crown is about 11 feet long (3.5 meters).
- To change a fraction to a decimal, divide the numerator by the denominator. A calculator can come in handy in some cases.

Example: $\frac{3}{7} \approx 0.428 \approx 0.4$

To Do List

- The chart here gives you the height of the statue from head to toe. Find and record your height on the chart. You can record your height to the nearest foot or in decimal form (e.g., 4' 6" = 4.5').
- Find and record your other measurements on the chart.
- Compare your height to the statue's height. How many times larger is the statue? Use this comparison to figure out your personal statue's other measurements.
- Calculate and record the other measurements of your personal Statue of Liberty.

Extra: Make a scale drawing of the head, right arm, and hand of your personal Statue of Liberty using the measurements in your table. Scale: 1 cm = 2 ft (or 1 cm = 6 cm).

	Measurements of Your Personal Statue of Liberty	Your Actual Measurements
Height, head to toe	111 ft (33.83 m or 3383 cm)	
Height of head		
Head, from ear to ear		
Length of right arm		
Length of hand		
Length of index finger		
Length and width of fingernail		
Width of eyes		
Width of mouth		
Length of nose		

CHAPTER 14
Battle at the Ballot Box

WOMEN AND THE RIGHT TO VOTE

Copyright © Good Year Books

Battle at the Ballot Box

WOMEN AND THE RIGHT TO VOTE

The Challenge

Students will take a closer look at the history of woman's suffrage. They make a map showing the date each state (or territory) gave women the vote. Next, for specific years listed, they find the fraction and/or percentage of states (or territories) that allowed women the right to vote. Finally, they write about all their results.

Extra: Students analyze their results in detail and gather data about the Equal Rights Amendment.

Math Skills/Concepts

fractions
decimals
percents (if students are ready)

Materials

calculator

Background: Women Behind the Suffrage Movement

Lucretia Mott, a Quaker and a great moral thinker, inspired Elizabeth Cady Stanton when the two met at a World Anti-Slavery Convention in 1840. Stanton and Mott organized the Seneca Falls conference, where Stanton shocked everyone by going so far as to include women's right to vote as one of the goals.

Lucy Stone, known for her powerful speechmaking, had struggled with her father as a young woman for the right to attend college. She ended up as head of the American Woman Suffrage Association.

Susan B. Anthony, born a Quaker, was a great organizer. Once she met Elizabeth Cady Stanton,

they worked together for the rest of their lives. She was arrested and fined for voting in 1872, and she acted as president of the National Woman Suffrage Association and later the National American Woman Suffrage Association. Hers is the only female image pictured on a U. S. coin (worth $1 and minted in 1979 and 1980).

Sojourner Truth also spoke out for both African American and white women's right to vote. "I wish woman to have her voice," she said.

As president of the National American Woman Suffrage Association, Carrie Chapman Catt put together a "Winning Plan" to get the Nineteenth Amendment passed by 1920. At the same time, Alice Paul used more militant tactics, such as marches and picketing, which resulted in arrests and imprisonment of women.

With the help of all these women and more, 26 million women voted in the 1920 presidential election.

In 1992 and 1996 women voters also made a noticeable difference, electing record numbers of women to Congress and supporting William Clinton over Robert Dole. Gloria Steinem voiced the goal of electing a half-female Congress and a woman president. A continuing constitutional challenge for women is winning passage of the Equal Rights Amendment.

Possible Solutions to the Challenge

• From their maps, students may conclude that the West was the first to allow woman's suffrage, that the East and Midwest came next, and that the South came last.

• These fractions, decimals, and percents showing how many of the 50 states (and territories) allowed woman's suffrage, by year. On their charts, students may notice a large gap between 1896 and 1910 and a significant increase in states allowing suffrage starting in 1917.

Questions

• How can you change a fraction to a decimal or a percent? (Divide the numerator by the denominator to get the decimal, and then move the decimal point two places to the right for the percent. Or divide the numerator by the denominator and press the % sign on the calculator.)

• How will your map show three different stages in the history of the woman's suffrage movement? (Students can use different colors or patterns, such as hatch marks.)

• From your map, what can you say in general about the geography of the woman's suffrage movement? (Woman's suffrage came first in the West, later in the East and Midwest, and after 1920 in the South.)

Extra:

• Were there any gaps in time as women gained the right to vote around the country?

(1896–1910 and 1914–1917)

• Were there any turning points or surges in the number of states granting voting rights to women? (1896, first territory to give voting rights; 1910, voting rights passed again after a fourteen-year gap; 1917–1919, many states from the East and Midwest allowed women to vote)

Date	Fraction	Decimal (Divide numerator by denominator.)	Percent
1869	$\frac{1}{48}$	0.02	2%
1870	$\frac{2}{48}$	0.04	4%
1893	$\frac{3}{49}$	0.06	6%
1896	$\frac{4}{50}$	0.08	8%
1910	$\frac{5}{50}$	0.10	10%
1911	$\frac{6}{50}$	0.12	12%
1913	$\frac{11}{50}$	0.22	22%
1914	$\frac{13}{50}$	0.26	26%
1917	$\frac{18}{50}$	0.36	36%
1918	$\frac{23}{50}$	0.46	46%
1919	$\frac{30}{50}$	0.60	60%

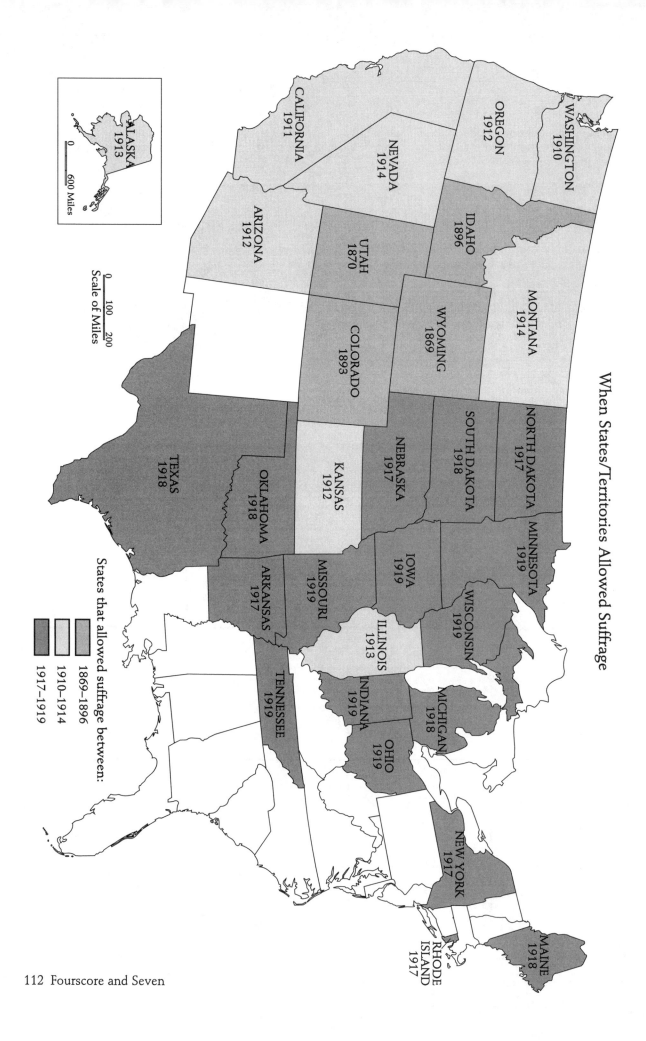

When States/Territories Allowed Suffrage

ALASKA
1913

0 ————— 600 Miles

0 —— 100 —— 200
Scale of Miles

WASHINGTON
1910

OREGON
1912

CALIFORNIA
1911

NEVADA
1914

IDAHO
1896

MONTANA
1914

ARIZONA
1912

UTAH
1870

WYOMING
1869

COLORADO
1893

NORTH DAKOTA
1917

SOUTH DAKOTA
1918

MINNESOTA
1919

NEBRASKA
1917

KANSAS
1912

TEXAS
1918

OKLAHOMA
1918

ARKANSAS
1917

MISSOURI
1919

IOWA
1919

WISCONSIN
1919

ILLINOIS
1913

INDIANA
1919

MICHIGAN
1918

OHIO
1919

TENNESSEE
1919

NEW YORK
1917

MAINE
1918

RHODE
ISLAND
1917

States that allowed suffrage between:

1869–1896

1910–1914

1917–1919

Copyright © Good Year Books

Battle at the Ballot Box

WOMEN AND THE RIGHT TO VOTE

 (EQUAL SUFFRAGE LEAGUE / HELP US WIN THE VOTE / VOTES FOR WOMEN)

Introduction

"Women have suffered agony of soul which you never can comprehend, that you and your daughters might inherit political freedom. That vote has been costly. Prize it!"
Carrie Chapman Catt, September 4, 1920*

* Marlene Targ Brill, *Let Women Vote!* Brookfield, CT: The Millbrook Press, 1996, p. 13.

Women and the Right to Vote 113

The battle for women's right to vote (or suffrage) began in 1848 and was finally won in 1920. In 1848, the first woman's rights convention was held in Seneca Falls, New York. Three hundred participants attended: women dressed in long, tight-waisted dresses, and some male supporters.

Over the next 20 years, suffragists held meetings, circulated petitions, made speeches, and wrote articles. Yet, in 1868 the Fourteenth Amendment to the Constitution of the United States dealt a serious blow to women's rights. African American men were given the vote, but women were still excluded.

Two competing women's organizations were formed in 1869, the more radical headed by Susan B. Anthony and Elizabeth Cady Stanton. Then in 1878, a California senator introduced the Anthony Amendment to Congress for the first time. The amendment, which stated, "The right of citizens of the United States to vote shall not be denied or abridged by the United States or by any state on account of sex," was soundly defeated.

In 1869 the territory of Wyoming was the first place in the United States to allow women to vote. But by the end of 1896, women could vote in only four states, and it was 14 more years before the fifth state gave voting rights to women. In the meantime, the two women's organizations joined forces. The movement focused more on voting rights, and it began to appeal to working class women. In the early 1900s, both Stanton and Anthony died, and the movement passed into new hands.

The movement gained momentum with the help of more aggressive methods (marching, picketing, and meeting with the president), more women in the work force during World War I, and a general change in people's thinking. Finally, in 1919, the Nineteenth Amendment (giving women the vote) was ratified by a vote of 274 to 136. On August 26, 1920, with a fight to the end, it was adopted by the states. From start to finish, it took 78 years for women to win the right to vote! "Prize it!"

The Challenge

Take a closer look at the history of woman's suffrage. Make a map showing the date each state (or territory) allowed women to vote. Next, for each year listed, find the fraction or percentage of states (or territories) that allowed women the right to vote. Write about your results. **Extra:** Analyze your results in detail. Gather data about the Equal Rights Amendment.

What You Will Need

calculator
chart on page 116

The Facts

This list of years (before 1920) shows when different states or territories gave women voting rights. Some states gave full suffrage, some presidential suffrage, and some primary election suffrage.

1869	Wyoming*
1870	Utah*
1893	Colorado
1896	Idaho
1910	Washington
1911	California
1912	Kansas, Oregon, Arizona
1913	Alaska,* Illinois
1914	Montana, Nevada
1917	New York, Nebraska, North Dakota, Rhode Island, Arkansas
1918	Michigan, Oklahoma, South Dakota, Maine, Texas
1919	Minnesota, Wisconsin, Iowa, Missouri, Indiana, Ohio, Tennessee

Wyoming, Utah, and Alaska were territories when they first allowed women to vote.

To Do List

- Make a map showing the dates each state (or territory) allowed woman suffrage.
  On the map, find a visual way to show which states allowed suffrage
       Between 1890 and 1896
       Between 1910 and 1914
       Between 1917 and 1919
  Be sure to include a key on your map.
- What do you notice about the map you've made? Write about any patterns you see.
- For each year that one or more states allowed women the right to vote, calculate the percentage of states (out of 50 states and territories, in most cases) where women could vote. Note that your teacher might want you to find fractions and/or decimals instead of percents. Fill in the chart on page 116 to record your findings. Notice that the total number of states and territories varies in the beginning of the chart.
- Study your chart. Write about anything you notice.

Extra:
- Look again at the list showing when different states and territories allowed woman's suffrage. How much time passed between each date? How many states were included for each date? When were the turning points? When did important changes occur? Analyze and write about the woman's suffrage movement using this list.
- Draw any other conclusions about the history of the woman's suffrage movement from the list, your map, and your chart of fractions and percentages.

Date	Fraction	Decimal (Divide numerator by denominator.)	Percent
1869	$\dfrac{1}{48}$	0.02	2%
1870	$\dfrac{\quad}{48}$		
1893	$\dfrac{\quad}{49}$		
1896	$\dfrac{\quad}{50}$		
1910	$\dfrac{\quad}{50}$		
1911	$\dfrac{\quad}{50}$		
1913	$\dfrac{\quad}{50}$		
1914	$\dfrac{\quad}{50}$		
1917	$\dfrac{\quad}{50}$		
1918	$\dfrac{\quad}{50}$		
1919	$\dfrac{\quad}{50}$		

CHAPTER 15
"I Do Solemnly Swear . . ."

PRESIDENTS OF THE UNITED STATES

"I Do Solemnly Swear . . ."
PRESIDENTS OF THE UNITED STATES

The Challenge

Students take a detailed look at the presidents of the United States. They choose a particular set of data having to do with the presidency, such as birthplace or age. Then they make a bar graph showing this data. Before graphing, they predict what they think the graph will look like.

Extra: Students make a double bar graph rather than a single bar graph of the data. Their double bar graph might show how the data looks for the first half of the presidents and how it looks for the second half of the presidents (or how it looks for Democrats and for Republicans).

Math Skills/Concepts
bar graphs
interpreting graphs

Materials
calculator

Background: Quotes from Some of the Presidents

"The basis of our political system is the right of the people to make and to alter their constitutions of government." *

After the inauguration: *"I greatly fear that my countrymen will expect too much from me."* †

George Washington

* Joseph R. Conlin, *The Morrow Book of Quotations in American History.* New York, NY: William Morrow and Company, 1984, p. 306.
† Paul F. Boller, Jr., *Presidential Anecdotes.* New York, NY: Oxford University Press, 1981, p. 20.

We hold these truths to be self-evident; that all men are created equal. . . ." ✱

On his death bed on the Fourth of July:
"This is the Fourth?" †

Thomas Jefferson

"As I would not be a slave, so I would not be a master." ✱

When he was called "two-faced," he said,
". . . If I had another face, do you think I would wear this one?. . . " †

"Fourscore and seven years ago our fathers brought forth on this continent, a new nation, conceived in liberty, and dedicated to the proposition that all men are created equal. Now we are engaged in a great civil war, testing whether that nation, or any nation so conceived, and so dedicated, can long endure." †

Abraham Lincoln
Gettysburg Address, November 1863

"Speak softly and carry a big stick. . . ." ✱

Of his daughter Alice: *"I can do one of two things. I can be President of the United States or I can control Alice. I cannot possibly do both."* †

Teddy Roosevelt

On entering World War I: *"It is a fearful thing to lead this great peaceful people into war. . . ."* ‡

Wilson liked to tell of a boy shoving his way through a large crowd gathered to hear Wilson: "Where is it? Where is it?" asked the boy. "Well, my boy, I guess I'm it," said Wilson. "Shucks," said the boy, "I thought it was a dogfight." †

Woodrow Wilson

"The only thing we have to fear is fear itself." ✱

On his polio: *"If you had spent two years in bed trying to wiggle your big toe, after that anything else would seem easy!"* †

Franklin Delano Roosevelt

". . . ask not what your country can do for you; ask what you can do for your country." °

On how he had become a war hero:
"It was absolutely involuntary. They sank my boat." †

John F. Kennedy

✱ Joseph R. Conlin, *The Morrow Book of Quotations in American History.* New York, NY: William Morrow and Company, 1984, pp. 156, 187, 252, 246.
† Paul F. Boller, Jr., *Presidential Anecdotes.* New York, NY: Oxford University Press, 1981, p. 39, 125, 206, 225, 266, 299.
‡ Elizabeth Frost, ed., *The Bully Pulpit.* New York: Facts on File, 1988, p. 257.
° John Bartlett, *Familiar Quotations,* 16th ed., by J. Boston: Little, Brown, 1992, p. 741.

Possible Solutions to the Challenge

This bar graph shows the ages of the presidents when they were inaugurated.

The ages range from 42 years old to 69 years old and nearly half of the Presidents were 51–55 years old.

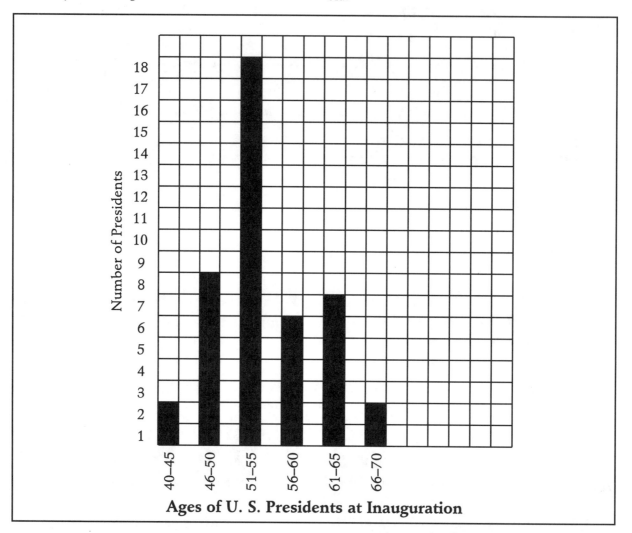

Ages of U. S. Presidents at Inauguration

Extra: The double bar graph on page 121 shows the birthplaces of the Presidents, grouped by regions of the country. Students may notice that many of the first Presidents came from the South and the East. Among later Presidents, more came from the Midwest and East, and a few from the West.

Note: If students need to group all the presidents into two parties for their double bar graph, they might find it helpful to know that the Federalists were the forerunners of the Republicans. The Democratic-Republican party became the Democratic party. Most Whigs became Republicans in the 1850s.

Questions

• What data will you graph? Do the categories need to be narrowed down? (Example: Presidents' ages could be in five- or ten-year spans. Birthplaces could be grouped by section of the country.)

• What do you predict your finished graph will look like?

• Would your graph make a better bar graph or pictograph?

• On your graph, do you see any patterns? highs? lows? unusual data?

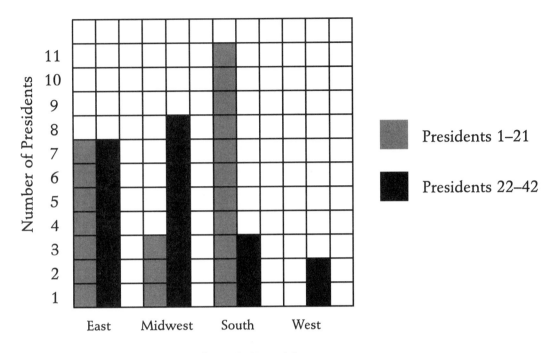

Birthplaces of U. S. Presidents

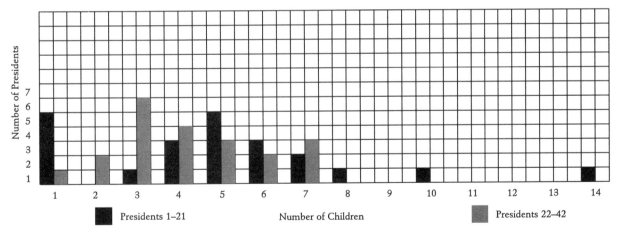

Number of Children of U. S. Presidents

Extra:

• Since your graph is a double bar graph, how will you show what each of the two bars stands for? (Make a color key for the bars on the graph.)

• How do the first half of the Presidents compare to the second half? Or how do the Democrats compare to the Republicans?

"I Do Solemnly Swear . . ."

PRESIDENTS OF THE UNITED STATES

Introduction

There are three qualifications for becoming president of the United States:

- You need to be at least 35 years old.
- You need to have lived in the United States for at least 14 years.

- You need to be a natural-born U. S. citizen.

The job pays $200,000 per year. The duties are to act as chief of state, head of the government, and commander-in-chief of the armed forces. If a president dies, resigns, or is removed from office, the vice-president is first in line to take over as president. Next come the Speaker of the House of Representatives, the president pro tempore of the Senate, and the secretary of state.

Though the office of president is open to anyone meeting the qualifications and wanting the job, all have had much in common in terms of race, gender, former occupation, and religion. The president has always belonged to one of two major political parties at the time.

But who knows what will happen in the next century? The closest a woman has come to being President is Madeleine Albright, the secretary of state under Bill Clinton, but she is not a natural-born citizen. In 1984 Geraldine Ferraro was the first woman running mate of a presidential candidate from a major political party. Polls in 1996 showed that if Colin Powell, an African American man, had run for president, he would have stood a good chance of winning.

Who would be your choice for a future President?

The Challenge

You will be taking a detailed look at the presidents of the United States. Choose a particular set of data having to do with the presidency, such as birthplace or age. Then make a bar graph showing this data. Before graphing, predict what you think the graph will look like.
Extra: Make a double bar graph instead of a single bar graph of the data. For example, you could show how the data looks for the first half of the presidents and how it looks for the second half of the presidents. Or show how the data looks for the Democrats and for the Republicans.

What You Will Need

graph paper

The Facts

Refer to the tables on the following pages.

Name	Birthplace _Date of Birth_	Date of Death _Age at Death_	Political Party	Dates Served _Age_	Occupation
1. George Washington	Westmoreland County, Va. _Feb. 22, 1732_	Dec. 14, 1799 _67_	Federalist*	1789–1797 _57–65_	planter, soldier
2. John Adams	Braintree, Mass. _Oct. 30, 1735_	July 4, 1826 _90_	Federalist*	1797–1801 _61–65_	lawyer, diplomat
3. Thomas Jefferson	Albemarle County, Va. _April 13, 1743_	July 4, 1826 _83_	Democratic Republican**	1801–1809 _57–65_	planter, lawyer
4. James Madison	Port Conway, Va. _Mar. 16, 1751_	June 28, 1836 _85_	Democratic Republican**	1809–1817 _58–66_	lawyer
5. James Monroe	Westmoreland County, Va. _April 28, 1758_	July 4, 1831 _73_	Democratic Republican**	1817–1825 _58–66_	lawyer
6. John Quincy Adams	Braintree, Mass. _July 11, 1767_	Feb. 23, 1848 _80_	Democratic Republican**	1825–1829 _57–61_	lawyer, diplomat
7. Andrew Jackson	Waxhaw settlement, S.C. _Mar. 15, 1767_	June 8, 1845 _78_	Democratic	1829–1837 _61–69_	lawyer, soldier
8. Martin Van Buren	Kinderhook, N.Y. _Dec. 5, 1782_	July 24, 1862 _79_	Democratic	1837–1841 _54–59_	lawyer
9. William H. Harrison	Berkeley, Va. _Feb. 9, 1773_	April 4, 1841 _68_	Whig***	1841 _68_	soldier, farmer
10. John Tyler	Greenway, Va. _Mar. 29, 1790_	Jan. 18, 1862 _71_	Whig***	1841–1845 _51–54_	lawyer
11. James K. Polk	near Pineville, N.C. _Nov. 2, 1795_	June 15, 1849 _53_	Democratic	1845–1849 _49–53_	lawyer
12. Zachary Taylor	Orange County, Va. _Nov. 24, 1784_	July 9, 1850 _65_	Whig***	1849–1850 _64–65_	soldier
13. Millard Fillmore	Locke, N.Y. _Jan. 7, 1800_	Mar. 8, 1874 _74_	Whig***	1850–1853 _50–53_	lawyer, teacher
14. Franklin Pierce	Hillsboro, N.H. _Nov. 23, 1804_	Oct. 8, 1869 _64_	Democratic	1853–1857 _48–52_	lawyer

Name	Birthplace *Date of Birth*	Date of Death *Age at Death*	Political Party	Dates Served *Age*	Occupation
15. James Buchanan	near Mercersburg, Pa. *April 23, 1791*	June 1, 1868 *77*	Democratic	1857–1861 *65–69*	lawyer, diplomat
16. Abraham Lincoln	near Hodgenville, Ky. *Feb. 12, 1809*	April 15, 1865 *56*	Republican	1861–1865 *52–56*	lawyer
17. Andrew Johnson	Raleigh, N.C. *Dec. 29, 1808*	July 31, 1875 *66*	Democratic	1865–1869 *56–60*	tailor
18. Ulysses S. Grant	Point Pleasant, Ohio *April 27, 1822*	July 23, 1885 *63*	Republican	1869–1877 *46–54*	soldier
19. Rutherford B. Hayes	Delaware, Ohio *Oct. 4, 1822*	Jan. 17, 1893 *70*	Republican	1877–1881 *54–58*	lawyer
20. James A. Garfield	Orange, Ohio *Nov. 19, 1831*	Sept. 19, 1881 *49*	Republican	1881 *49–49*	lawyer, teacher
21. Chester A. Arthur	Fairfield, Vt. *Oct. 5, 1829*	Nov. 18, 1886 *57*	Republican	1881–1885 *51–55*	lawyer, teacher
22. Grover Cleveland	Caldwell, N.J. *Mar. 18, 1837*	June 24, 1908 *71*	Democratic	1885–1889 *47–51*	lawyer
23. Benjamin Harrison	North Bend, Ohio *Aug. 20, 1833*	Mar. 13, 1901 *67*	Republican	1889–1893 *55–59*	lawyer
22. Grover Cleveland	Caldwell, N.J. *Mar. 18, 1837*	June 24, 1908 *71*	Democratic	1893–1897 *55–59*	lawyer
25. William McKinley	Niles, Ohio *Jan. 29, 1843*	Sept. 14, 1901 *58*	Republican	1897–1901 *54–58*	lawyer
26. Theodore Roosevelt	New York, N.Y. *Oct. 27, 1858*	Jan. 6, 1919 *60*	Republican	1901–1909 *42–50*	author, soldier
27. William H. Taft	Cincinnati, Ohio *Sept. 15, 1857*	Mar. 8, 1930 *72*	Republican	1909–1913 *51–55*	lawyer
28. Woodrow Wilson	Staunton, Va. *Dec. 29, 1856*	Feb. 3, 1924 *67*	Democratic	1913–1921 *56–64*	educator

Name	Birthplace / Date of Birth	Date of Death / Age at Death	Political Party	Dates Served / Age	Occupation
29. Warren G. Harding	near Blooming Grove, Ohio / Nov. 2, 1865	Aug. 2, 1923 / 57	Republican	1921–1923 / 55–57	editor
30. Calvin Coolidge	Plymouth Notch, Vt. / July 4, 1872	Jan. 5, 1933 / 60	Republican	1923–1929 / 51–56	lawyer
31. Herbert C. Hoover	West Branch, Iowa / Aug. 10, 1874	Oct. 20, 1964 / 90	Republican	1929–1933 / 54–58	engineer
32. Franklin D. Roosevelt	Hyde Park, N.Y. / Jan. 30, 1882	April 12, 1945 / 63	Democratic	1933–1945 / 51–63	lawyer
33. Harry S. Truman	Lamar, Mo. / May 8, 1884	Dec. 26, 1972 / 88	Democratic	1945–1953 / 60–68	farmer, haberdasher
34. Dwight D. Eisenhower	Denison, Tex. / Oct.14, 1890	Mar. 28, 1969 / 78	Republican	1953–1961 / 62–70	soldier
35. John F. Kennedy	Brookline, Mass. / May 29, 1917	Nov. 22, 1963 / 46	Democratic	1961–1963 / 43–46	author
36. Lyndon B. Johnson	Stonewall, Tex. / Aug. 27, 1908	Jan. 22, 1973 / 64	Democratic	1963–1969 / 55–60	teacher
37. Richard M. Nixon	Yorba Linda, Calif. / Jan. 9, 1913	April 22, 1994 / 81	Republican	1969–1974 / 56–61	lawyer
38. Gerald R. Ford	Omaha, Nebr. / July 14, 1913		Republican	1974–1977 / 61–63	lawyer
39. Jimmy Carter	Plains, Ga. / Oct. 1, 1924		Democratic	1977–1981 / 52–56	farmer, businessman
40. Ronald W. Reagan	Tampico, Ill. / Feb. 6, 1911		Republican	1981–1989 / 69–77	actor
41. George H.W. Bush	Milton, Mass. / June 12, 1924		Republican	1989–1993 / 64–69	businessman
42. William J. Clinton	Hope, Ark. / Aug. 19, 1946		Democratic	1993– / 46	lawyer

*Federalist Party is forerunner of the Republican Party.
**Democratic-Republican Party became the Democratic Party.
***Most Whigs became Republicans.

Name	College	Religion	Wife *Number of Children*	Loser in Election	Vice-President
1. George Washington		Episcopalian	Martha (Dandridge) Custis, *0*	John Adams	John Adams
2. John Adams	Harvard	Unitarian	Abigail Smith, *F-2, M-3*	Thomas Jefferson	Thomas Jefferson
3. Thomas Jefferson	William and Mary	attended Unitarian & Episcopal	Martha (Wayles) Skelton, *F-5, M-1*	Aaron Burr, Charles C. Pinckney	Aaron Burr, George Clinton
4. James Madison	Princeton	Episcopalian	Dolley (Payne) Todd, *0*	Charles C. Pinckney, De Witt Clinton	George Clinton, Elbridge Gerry
5. James Monroe	William and Mary	Episcopalian	Elizabeth Kortright, *F-2, M-1*	Rufus King no opponent	Daniel D. Tompkins
6. John Quincy Adams	Harvard	Unitarian	Louisa Catherine Johnson, *F-1, M-3*	Andrew Jackson	John C. Calhoun
7. Andrew Jackson		Presbyterian	Rachel (Donelson) Robards, *0*	John Quincy Adams, Henry Clay	John C. Calhoun, Martin Van Buren
8. Martin Van Buren		Dutch Reformed	Hannah Hoes, *M-4*	William H. Harrison	Richard M. Johnson
9. William H. Harrison	Hampden-Sydney	Episcopalian	Anna Symmes, *F-4, M-6*	Martin Van Buren	John Tyler
10. John Tyler	William and Mary	Episcopalian	Letitia Christian, Julia Gardiner, *F-6, M-8*		
11. James K. Polk	U. of North Carolina	Methodist	Sarah Childress, *0*	Henry Clay	George M. Dallas
12. Zachary Taylor		Episcopalian	Margaret Mackall Smith, *F-5, M-1*	Lewis Cass	Millard Fillmore
13. Millard Fillmore		Unitarian	Abigail Powers, Caroline (Carmichael) McIntosh, *F-1, M-1*		
14. Franklin Pierce	Bowdoin	Episcopalian	Jane Means Appleton, *M-3*	Winfield Scott	William R. King

Name	College	Religion	Wife *Number of Children*	Loser in Election	Vice-President
15. James Buchanan	Dickinson	Presbyterian	Unmarried, *0*	John C. Frémont	John C. Breckinridge
16. Abraham Lincoln		attended Presbyterian	Mary Todd, *M-4*	Stephen A. Douglas, George B. McClellan	Hannibal Hamlin, Andrew Johnson
17. Andrew Johnson		Methodist	Eliza McCardle, *F-2, M-3*		
18. Ulysses S. Grant	U.S. Military Academy	Methodist	Julia Boggs Dent, *F-1, M-3*	Horatio Seymour, Horace Greeley	Schuyler Colfax, Henry Wilson
19. Rutherford B. Hayes	Kenyon	attended Methodist	Lucy Ware Webb, *F-1, M-7*	Samuel J. Tilden	William A. Wheeler
20. James A. Garfield	Williams	Disciples of Christ	Lucretia Rudolph, *F-1, M-4*	Winfield S. Hancock	Chester A. Arthur
21. Chester A. Arthur	Union	Episcopalian	Ellen Lewis Herndon, *F-1, M-2*		
22. Grover Cleveland		Presbyterian	Frances Folsom, *F-3, M-2*	James G. Blaine	Thomas A. Hendricks
23. Benjamin Harrison	Miami	Presbyterian	Caroline Lavinia Scott, Mary Scott (Lord) Dimmick, *F-2, M-1*	Grover Cleveland	Levi P. Morton
24. Grover Cleveland		Presbyterian	Frances Folsom, *F-3, M-2*	Benjamin Harrison	Adlai E. Stevenson
25. William McKinley	Allegheny College	Methodist	Ida Saxton, *F-2*	William J. Bryan	Garrett A. Hobart, Theodore Roosevelt
26. Theodore Roosevelt	Harvard	Dutch Reformed	Alice Hathaway Lee, Edith Kermit Carow, *F-2, M-4*	Alton B. Parker	Charles W. Fairbanks
27. William H. Taft	Yale	Unitarian	Helen Herron, *F-1, M-2*	William J. Bryan	James S. Sherman
28. Woodrow Wilson	Princeton	Presbyterian	Ellen Louise Axson, Edith (Bolling) Galt, *F-3*	Theodore Roosevelt, Charles E. Hughes	Thomas R. Marshall

Name	College	Religion	Wife Number of Children	Loser in Election	Vice-President
29. Warren G. Harding		Baptist	Florence (King) De Wolfe, *0*	James M. Cox	Calvin Coolidge
30. Calvin Coolidge	Amherst	Congregationalist	Grace Anna Goodhue, *M-2*	John W. Davis	Charles G. Dawes
31. Herbert C. Hoover	Stanford	Friends (Quaker)	Lou Henry, *M-2*	Alfred E. Smith	Charles Curtis
32. Franklin D. Roosevelt	Harvard	Episcopalian	Anna Eleanor Roosevelt, *F-1, M-5*	Herbert Hoover, Alfred M. Landon, Wendell L. Willkie, Thomas E. Dewey	John N. Garner, Henry A. Wallace, Harry S. Truman
33. Harry S. Truman		Baptist	Elizabeth Virginia Wallace, *F-1*	Thomas E. Dewey	Alben W. Barkley
34. Dwight D. Eisenhower	U.S. Military Academy	Presbyterian	Mamie Geneva Doud, *M-2*	Adlai E. Stevenson	Richard M. Nixon
35. John F. Kennedy	Harvard	Roman Catholic	Jacqueline Bouvier, *F-1, M-2*	Richard M. Nixon	Lyndon B. Johnson
36. Lyndon B. Johnson	Southwest Texas State	Disciples of Christ	Claudia Alta "Lady Bird" Taylor, *F-2*	Barry M. Goldwater	Hubert H. Humphrey
37. Richard M. Nixon	Whittier	Friends (Quaker)	Thelma Patricia Ryan, *F-2*	Hubert H. Humphrey, George S. McGovern	Spiro T. Agnew, Gerald R. Ford
38. Gerald R. Ford	Michigan	Episcopalian	Elizabeth Bloomer, *F-1, M-3*		Nelson A. Rockefeller
39. Jimmy Carter	U.S. Naval Academy	Baptist	Rosalynn Smith, *F-1, M-3*	Gerald R. Ford	Walter F. Mondale
40. Ronald W. Reagan	Eureka	Disciples of Christ	Jane Wyman, Nancy Davis, *F-2, M-2*	Jimmy Carter, Walter F. Mondale	George H. W. Bush
41. George H. W. Bush	Yale	Episcopalian	Barbara Pierce, *F-2, M-4*	Michael S. Dukakis	Dan Quayle
42. William J. Clinton	Georgetown	Baptist	Hillary Rodham, *F-1*	George H. W. Bush	Al Gore

To Do List

- Look at the facts about the presidents and come up with a set of data to graph.
- Group your data, if necessary. For example, it isn't practical to include a bar on the graph for every president's birthplace or every president's age at inauguration. How could birthplaces be grouped? How about ages?
- Predict and write about how you think your graph will turn out.
- Graph your data on a bar graph.
- Analyze the bar graph and write about your conclusions.
- Ideas for graphs: age at inauguration, occupation, place of birth, age at death, religion, number of male and female children, political party, how many losers in an election later became president, how many vice-presidents became president.
- Interesting idea to be researched: each President's birth order in his family.

Extra:
- Make a double bar graph from your data. For example, you could show how the data looks for the first half of the presidents and how it looks for the second half of the presidents. (If there is an uneven number of presidents, use the data for Grover Cleveland only once, since he served as the twenty-second and twenty-fourth president.) Or you could show how the data looks for the Democrats and for the Republicans.
- Make a key to your double bar graph. For example, the bar on the graph for the first half of the presidents could be red and the bar for the most recent half of the presidents could be blue.
- How do the first half of the presidents compare to the second half? (Or how do the Democrats compare to the Republicans?)
- Analyze the graph and write about your conclusions.

CHAPTER 16

Which Faces Do You Recognize?

CURRENT EVENTS

131

Which Faces Do You Recognize?

CURRENT EVENTS

The Challenge

All students bring in a picture of a political figure from the newspaper. These are numbered and passed around. Each student writes down the name of anyone he or she recognizes. Class members introduce each person pictured and circulate the pictures again for students to identify. Students figure out the percent they identified correctly in each round.

Extra: Students figure what percent of the pictures show women, men, and people of different ethnic backgrounds.

Math Skills/Concepts

percents
fractions and decimals (if students aren't ready for percents)

Materials

calculator

Possible Solutions to the Challenge

Students will compare the number they got correct over the total number of pictures to get a fraction. They can divide the numerator by the denominator and press the % key on the calculator. Or they can divide the numerator by the denominator to get a decimal. By moving the decimal point two places to the right, they get a percent.

Questions

• Why does it help to recognize people in the news?
• How can you figure percents correctly?
Extra: What percentage of the pictures show women, men, people of different ethnic backgrounds?

Which Faces Do You Recognize?

CURRENT EVENTS

Introduction

Men and women in U. S. politics interact with people from all over the world. Keeping up with current events in newspapers and magazines is a lot more interesting if you recognize the people pictured in the news.

The Challenge

Everyone in the class needs to bring in a picture of a political figure from the newspaper. Number the pictures, pass them around, and let everyone write

To Do List

- Each person in the class should cut out a picture of a politician from a newspaper or magazine. Make sure there is a good representation of gender, race, and age.
- Write a few sentences about your person and his or her job.
- Number all the pictures.
- Pass the pictures around and have everyone write down the names of the people he or she recognizes.
- Have each student in the class introduce the person in his or her picture.
- Calculate the percent you named correctly.
- Pass around the pictures again.
- Calculate the percent you named correctly this time.

down the name of anyone he or she recognizes. Have class members introduce each person pictured, and pass the pictures around again. Figure out what percentage you identified correctly in each round.

Extra: Figure out what percentage of the pictures show women, men, and people of different ethnic backgrounds.

What You Will Need

calculator

Bibliography

Weaving with Spider Woman: Navajo Blankets

Amsden, Charles Avery. *Navaho Weaving.* Santa Ana, CA: The Fine Arts Press, 1934.

Berlant, Anthony, and Mary Hunt Kahlenberg. *Walk in Beauty: The Navajo and Their Blankets.* Boston: New York Graphic Society, 1977.

Doherty, Craig A., and Katherine M. Doherty. *The Apaches and Navajos.* New York: Franklin Watts, 1989.

Edmonds, Margot, and Ella E. Clark. *Voices of the Winds.* New York: Facts on File, 1989.

Franco, Betsy. *TexTile Math.* Mountain View, CA: Creative Publications, 1996.

James, George Wharton. *Indian Blankets and Their Makers, The Navajo.* Glorieta, NM: The Rio Grande Press, 1974.

Kahlenberg, Mary Hunt, and Anthony Berlant. *The Navajo Blanket,* New York: Praeger Publishers, Inc., 1972.

"Navajo Textiles 1995 Calendar." Natural History Museum of Los Angeles County, 1995.

Snyder, George. "Woven to the Earth." *San Francisco Chronicle,* May 4, 1997; sec. A1, 4–5.

From Triumph to Tragedy: Réne-Robert Cavalier, Sieur de La Salle, French Explorer

Hargrove, Jim. *René-Robert Cavalier Sieur de La Salle.* Chicago: Childrens Press, 1990.

Knight, Frank. *Stories of Famous Explorers by Land.* Philadelphia: The Westminster Press, 1945.

Laroe, Lisa Moore. "La Salle's Last Voyage." *National Geographic,* May 1997; 72–83.

Muhlstein, Anka. *La Salle, Explorer of the North American Frontier.* New York: Arcade Publishing, 1994.

Roberts, David. "Sieur de La Salle's Fateful Landfall." *Smithsonian,* April 1997; 40–52.

Terrell, John Upton. *La Salle: The Life and Times of an Explorer.* New York: Weybright and Talley, 1968.

Did Betsy Ross Really Sew It? The Stars and Stripes

Eggenberger, David. *Flags of the U.S.A.* New York: Thomas Y. Crowell, 1959.

Mastai, Boleslaw, and Marie-Louise D'Otrange Mastai. *The Stars and the Stripes.* New York: Alfred A. Knopf, 1973.

Parrish, Thomas. *The American Flag.* New York: Simon and Schuster, 1973.

Blending African and American Traditions: African American Quilters

Franco, Betsy. *TexTile Math.* Mountain View, CA: Creative Publications, 1996.

Freeman, Roland L. *A Communion of the Spirits.* Nashville: Rutledge Hill Press, 1996.

Ringgold, Faith. *Tar Beach.* New York: Crown Publishers, 1991.

Wahlman, Maude Southwell. *Signs and Symbols, African Images in African-American Quilts.* New York: Studio Books, 1993.

Sheepes Tongue Pie: A Selection of Colonial Recipes

1776, A Collection of Traditional Early American Recipes Updated for Today's Taste. Liberty, MO: Nightlife Magazine, 1975.

Barck, Oscar Theodore, Jr. *Colonial America.* Toronto: Macmillan, 1958.

Earle, Alice (Morse). *Home Life in Colonial Days.* New York: Macmillan, 1898.

_____. *Home and Child Life in Colonial Days.* New York: Macmillan, 1969.

Gould, Mary Earle. *The Early American House.* Rutland, VT: Charles E. Tuttle, 1965.

Hess, Karen. *Martha Washington's Booke of Cookery.* New York: Columbia University Press, 1981.

"Boston Harbor a teapot tonight!": The Boston Tea Party

Boston Tea Party Ship and Museum. Congress Street on Harbor Walk, Pier 1, Pratt St., Boston, MA, 02210. Tel. 617-338-1773.

Chidsey, Donald Barr. *The Great Separation: The Story of the Boston Tea Party and the Beginning of the American Revolution.* New York: Crown Publishers, 1965.

Cooke, Alistair. *America.* New York: Alfred A. Knopf, 1974.

Griswold, Wesley S. *The Night the Revolution Began.* Brattleboro, VT: The Stephen Greene Press, 1972.

Phelan, Mary Kay. *The Story of the Boston Tea Party.* New York: Thomas Y. Crowell, 1973.

Young, Alfred F., and Terry J. Fife, with Mary E. Janzen. *We the People.* Philadelphia: Temple University Press, 1993.

From Licorice to Button Hooks: Shopping at a General Store

Carson, Gerald. *The Old Country Store.* New York: Oxford University Press, 1954.

Coffin, Margaret M. *Death in Early America,* New York: Thomas Nelson, Inc., 1976.

Earle, Alice (Morse). *Home and Child Life in Colonial Days.* New York: Macmillan, 1969.

Green, George B. Account Book from General Store, 1827–1849. Windsor, VT. Library of Sturbridge Village, Sturbridge, MA.

Roberts, Bruce, and Ray Jones. *American Country Stores.* Chester, CT: The Globe Pequot Press, 1991.

Wigginton, Eliot, and Margie Bennett, ed. *Foxfire 9.* Garden City, NY: Anchor Press/Doubleday, 1986.

Wagons Ho! Packing a Covered Wagon

Book of Remembrance, a Mormon family diary.

Butruille, Susan G. *Women's Voices from the Oregon Trail.* Boise: Tamarack Books, 1993.

Florin, Lambert. *Western Wagon Wheels.* Seattle: Superior Publishing Co., 1970.

Freedman, Russell. *Children of the Wild West.* New York: Clarion Books, 1983.

Holmes, Kennenth L., ed. and comp. *Covered Wagon Women: Diaries and Letters from the Western Trails, 1840–1849.* Lincoln: University of Nebraska Press, 1983.

Marcy, Randolph B. *The Prairie Traveler.* New York: The Berkley Publishing Group, 1993.

Old West Wagon Treks. Judy and Stan Mayo. Tel. 306–427–4499. Box 375, Shell Lake, SK SOJ 2GO, Canada.

Shumway, George; Edward Durell; and Howard C. Frey. *Conestoga Wagon 1750–1850.* Williamsburg, VA.: Early American Industries Association, 1964.

Walker, Henry Pickering. *The Wagonmasters.* Norman: University of Oklahoma Press, 1966.

Werner, Emmy E. *Pioneer Children on the Journey West.* Boulder, CO: Westview Press, 1995.

Home on the Range: The American Buffalo

Barsness, Larry. *Heads, Hides & Horns.* Fort Worth: Texas Christian University Press, 1985.

"Bison Slaughter Raises New Alarm About Herd's Survival." *San Francisco Chronicle,* Jan. 31, 1997; sec. A12.

Crozier-Hogle, Lois, and Darryl Babe Wilson. *Surviving in Two Worlds.* Austin: University of Texas Press, 1997.

Hodgson, Bryan. "Buffalo, Back Home on the Range." *National Geographic,* November 1994; 64–89.

"Homeless on the Range." *Newsweek,* March 17, 1997; 67.

National Bison Association, Denver, CO. 4701 Marion St., Denver, CO 80216. Tel. 303-292-2833

"White Magic." *People Weekly,* October 3, 1994; 52.

"Why Bison?" Web page, http://kitchen.homecom.com/the maestro/JH/Businesses/BH

Eureka! The California Gold Rush

Bauer, Helen. *California Gold Days.* Garden City, NY: Doubleday, 1954.

Clappe, Louise Amelia Knapp (Smith). *The Shirley Letters from the California Mines.* New York: Alfred A. Knopf, 1949.

Francl, Joseph. *The Overland Journey of Joseph Francl.* San Francisco: William P. Wreden, 1968.

Gintzler, A. S. *Rough and Ready Prospectors.* Santa Fe: John Muir Publications, 1994.

Levy, JoAnn. *They Saw the Elephant, Women in the California Gold Rush.* Hamden, CT: (Archon Books) The Shoe String Press, 1990.

Mattison, Elise. "A Chronicle of Pre-1848 California Gold Discoveries." *California Geology,* January/February 1996; 11–19.

Wilcox, Del. *Voyagers to California.* Elk, CA: Sea Rock Press, 1991.

Wyman, Walker D. *California Emigrant Letters.* New York: Bookman Associates Publishers, 1952.

A "Train" to Freedom: The Underground Railroad

Bentley, Judith. *Harriet Tubman.* New York: Franklin Watts, 1990.

Blockson, Charles L. *The Underground Railroad.* New York: Prentice Hall, 1987.

Hamilton, Virginia. *Many Thousand Gone.* New York: Alfred A. Knopf, 1993.

Haskins, Jim. *Get on Board: The Story of the Underground Railroad.* New York: Scholastic, 1993.

"History and Geography of the Underground Railroad" Web page, http://www.nps.gov/undergroundrr/history.htm.

Mallory, Maria. "Bound for Freedom." *U.S. News and World Report,* April 14, 1997; 78–83.

Cohen, Anthony. "Retracing the Route to Freedom." *National Parks,* November/December 1996; 40–43.

Siebert, Wilbur Henry. *The Mysteries of Ohio's Underground Railroad.* Columbus, OH: Long's College Book Company, 1951.

_____. *The Underground Railroad from Slavery to Freedom.* New York: The Macmillan Company, 1899.

Webster, Donovan. "Traveling the Long Road to Freedom, One Step at a Time." *Smithsonian,* October 1996; 48–60.

The Mail Must Go Through: The Pony Express

Dicerto, Joseph J. *The Pony Express, Hoofbeats in the Wilderness.* New York: Franklin Watts, 1989.

Settle, Raymond W. *Saddles and Spurs: The Pony Express Saga.* Harrisburg, PA: Stackpole, 1955.

Van Der Linde, Laurel. *The Pony Express.* New York: New Discovery Books, 1993.

Winther, Oscar Osburn. *Via Western Express and Stagecoach.* Stanford, CA: Stanford University Press, 1945.

Lady Liberty: Immigration and the Statue of Liberty

Bell, James B., and Richard I. Abrams. *In Search of Liberty.* Garden City, NY: Doubleday & Company, 1984.

Bode, Janet. *New Kids in Town.* New York: Scholastic, 1989.

Freedman, Russell. *Immigrant Kids.* New York: E. P. Dutton, 1980.

Handlin, Oscar. *A Pictorial History of Immigration.* New York: Crown Publishers, 1972.

Maestro, Betsy, and Giulio Maestro. *The Story of the Statue of Liberty.* New York: Lothrop, Lee & Shepard Books, 1986.

Shapiro, Mary J. *How They Built the Statue of Liberty.* New York: Random House, 1985.

Shapiro, William E. *The Statue of Liberty, A First Book.* New York: Franklin Watts, 1985.

White, Jack E. "I'm Just Who I Am." *Time* Magazine, May 5, 1997; 32–36.

Battle at the Ballot Box: Women and the Right to Vote

Brill, Marlene Targ. *Let Women Vote!* Brookfield, CT: The Millbrook Press, 1996.

Kendall, Martha E. *Susan B. Anthony.* Springfield, NJ: Enslow Publishers, 1997.

Kruman, Marc W. "Suffrage." *The Reader's Companion to American History.* Boston: Houghton-Mifflin, 1991; 1043–1047.

Sigerman, Harriet. *New Paths to Power, American Women 1890–1920,* vol. 6. New York: Oxford University Press, 1994.

Smith, Karen Manners. *New Paths to Power, American Women 1890–1920,* vol. 7. New York: Oxford University Press, 1994.

Sullivan, George. *The Day the Women Got the Vote.* New York: Scholastic, 1994.

Tierney, Helen, ed. *Women's Studies Encyclopedia.* vol. 3. *History, Philosophy, and Religion.* New York: Greenwood Press, 1991.

The World Book Encyclopedia. 1996 ed., vol. 21; "Woman Suffrage."

"I Do Solemnly Swear . . ."; Presidents of the United States

Bartlett, John, ed. *Familiar Quotations.* Boston: Little, Brown and Company, 1992.

Bassett, Margaret. *Profiles & Portraits of American Presidents & Their Wives.* Freeport, ME: The Bond Wheelwright Company, 1969.

Boller, Paul F. *Presidential Anecdotes.* New York: Oxford University Press, 1981.

Collier's Encyclopedia. 1986 edition, vol. 19; "Presidents of the United States."

Conlin, Joseph R. *The Morrow Book of Quotations in American History.* New York: William Morrow and Company, 1984.

Frost, Elizabeth, ed. *The Bully Pulpit, Quotations from America's Presidents.* New York: Facts on File Publications, 1988.

The Grolier Multimedia Encyclopedia [CD-ROM]. "Bill Clinton." Grolier Electronic Publishing, 1994.

Ragsdale, Lyn. *Vital Satistics on the Presidency, Washington to Clinton.* Washington, DC: Congressional Quarterly Inc., 1996.

The World Book Encyclopedia. 1990 edition, vol. 15; "Presidents of the United States."